The Principal Coaching Model

The Principal Coaching Model

How to Plan, Design, and Implement a Successful Program

Larry Hausner

ROWMAN & LITTLEFIELD
Lanham • Boulder • New York • London

Published by Rowman & Littlefield
An imprint of The Rowman & Littlefield Publishing Group, Inc.
4501 Forbes Boulevard, Suite 200, Lanham, Maryland 20706
www.rowman.com

Unit A, Whitacre Mews, 26-34 Stannary Street, London SE11 4AB

Copyright © 2018 by Larry Hausner
All figures created by author.

All rights reserved. No part of this book may be reproduced in any form or by any electronic or mechanical means, including information storage and retrieval systems, without written permission from the publisher, except by a reviewer who may quote passages in a review.

British Library Cataloguing in Publication Information Available

Library of Congress Cataloging-in-Publication Data

Names: Hausner, Larry, 1967- author.
Title: The principal coaching model : how to plan, design, and implement a successful program / Larry Hausner.
Description: Lanham : Rowman & Littlefield, [2018] | Includes bibliographical references.
Identifiers: LCCN 2018022711 (print) | LCCN 2018032257 (ebook) | ISBN 9781475845556 (electronic) | ISBN 9781475845501 | ISBN 9781475845501 (cloth : alk. paper) | ISBN 9781475845518 (paper : alk. paper)
Subjects: LCSH: School principals—In-service training—United States. | Mentoring in education—United States.
Classification: LCC LB1738.5 (ebook) | LCC LB1738.5 .H38 2018 (print) | DDC 371.2/012—dc23
LC record available at https://lccn.loc.gov/2018022711

∞ ™ The paper used in this publication meets the minimum requirements of American National Standard for Information Sciences Permanence of Paper for Printed Library Materials, ANSI/NISO Z39.48-1992.

Printed in the United States of America

This book is a dedicated to my children, Riley and Jacob.
Everything I do, I do for them.
They are my world.

Contents

Foreword ix

Preface xi

Acknowledgments xiii

1 It's Lonely in the Middle 1
2 An Uncomfortable Reality —Now What? 11
3 What the Literature Says 19
4 What the Principals Have to Say 41
5 Case Studies 57
6 Best Practices, Proven Results, and Next Steps 77

References 89

About the Author 95

Foreword

As Dr. Hausner suggests, does principal coaching make a positive impact on student performance, improve school climate, and reduce principal turnover? Without question. As a former successful superintendent in numerous districts, I personally saw the effect providing principals with coaching has on the organization as whole. Today's principals are in high demand, being asked to lead bigger and better than before. School communities are ever changing and becoming more challenging to manage and the one-on-one, confidential coaching model of Dr. Hausner's is the answer to meet these demands.

In *The Principal Coaching Model*, Dr. Hausner takes the reader on a journey that provides the rationale, research, the input of principals, and worthy case study examples for districts to move forward with a coaching model or improve the one already in place. There may be other sources suggesting the value of coaching, but this book goes above and beyond with its depth and the culmination of Dr. Hausner's work with his Research-Based Implementation Model for principal coaching.

Districts often allocate resources providing instructional coaching to its support teachers. In addition, of late, there has been an increase in superintendents receiving coaching support by outside professionals as well. While these are sound, and often research based, practices, what is missing according to Dr. Hausner is principal coaching. I completely agree. The principalship has become an incredibly demanding position with increasing stressors from both inside and outside the school community. For principals to reach their potential, and stay in the job, coaching principals is the answer and for districts to support their principals with this sound practice is key. *The Principal Coaching Model* is the vehicle to make it happen.

In addition, his Research-Based Implementation Model of coaching not only provides districts with non-negotiables and optional practices, but it is also a proven winner and one that will deliver successful results to your district. Later in this book, those impressive results will be shared. As a former results-driven superintendent, I appreciate knowing that implementing Dr. Hausner's model has a track record of success.

The Principal Coaching Model is an excellent book that every principal, supervisor of principals, and district superintendent must read. It is time for district-level decision makers to implement Dr. Hausner's coaching model. The days of being considered a good principal because the school had a good band, athletic program, or choir are gone.

I have known Dr. Hausner since 2011. He was one of my doctoral students at the University of Southern California. After graduation, I recommended the university hire him as a adjunct professor. As the course lead, I noticed he quickly became an excellent professor and an asset to the program. In addition, I know Dr. Hausner to be one of the best principals I know because he understands teaching and learning. More importantly, he knows how to build capacity in his teaching staff through staff development, training, and coaching.

Today, as Dr. Hausner explains, being a principal is very complex and principals need support. Districts, as he mentions, need good staff development for their principals. They need an experienced coach who will listen, provide sound advice, and serve as a sounding board to the many challenges principals face.

I recommend this book, as Dr. Hausner explains, not only for principals but also for those aspiring to become principals. In *The Principal Coaching Model*, Dr. Hausner captures what principals need to be successful in the twenty-first century. Anyone who reads this book and applies the principles Dr. Hausner outlines should be a successful principal, have a very strong teaching staff, and more importantly know what to do when difficult situations arise.

Dr. Pedro E. Garcia
Superintendent, Nashville, TN (Retired)
Professor, Rossier School of Education,
University of Southern California (Retired)

Preface

After spending ten years as a sportscaster, I felt a calling to serve children. Even while broadcasting baseball games or hosting a television show, I always pictured myself in front of a classroom full of students. I felt I was needed to serve children. I experienced a calling, of sorts, and I chose education as a second career.

During the time I was in school earning a teaching credential, I could see my future in the role of principal as a goal even before my first day of teaching. I knew then that my purpose was, and still is, to make a positive difference in the lives of students every day. Writing this book is an avenue to support those who work for children every day, which is incredibly rewarding with the ultimate goal of helping children reach their potential through the adults that serve them.

As a K–12 public school educator for over twenty years, I have experience as a teacher, assistant principal, principal, coordinator, and cabinet-level director. For this book, two areas of my background make me uniquely qualified to undertake this project: One, my fourteen years of serving as a site principal, and two, my role as coach to school principals. Also, I have served as an adjunct professor of education in the doctoral program at the University of Southern California.

As stated above, I have served in the role as a principal coach. In early 2005, I was approached by a colleague who encouraged me to share with others my successes and impactful strategies that I implemented as a principal. After some soul searching, Coaching School Leadership was born. I decided to create a principal coaching model that I believed would lead to increased student performance through improved principal effectiveness. I brought this model to principals in Hawaii on the island of Maui.

Coaching School Leadership was my creation as I sought to not only share the innovative and creative programs of schools in which I served, but also and more importantly, to offer one-on-one, peer-to-peer principal coaching.

In the role of coach, I have been on the front lines with principals. I have seen the work they take on every day with enthusiasm and a heart for kids. I have also witnessed the value of coaching along with its impact on the effectiveness of principals improving student performance. Principals benefit from one-on-one, open, honest coaching that is not evaluative in nature. Providing this risk-free environment allow principals to speak freely with me knowing that I am truly there to support and coach them without them feeling vulnerable and judged. Once that trust was established, true progress was made (see chapter 6 and Proven Results).

My passion for the principalship, leadership, teaching, and learning has never been as important to me as it is today, twenty-plus years into my career. My purpose here is to support school leaders with practical, hands-on suggestions for practice to assist them in this demanding position that will hopefully lead to supporting their students, staffs, and communities while embracing and loving the job more than ever. It is a great job. It is the best I have had as an educator, but it is a difficult one and in most places a lonely job. It is time to recognize this and provide these principals support. The time is now.

It is clear that America needs the best and brightest to lead our schools. Our students, teachers, and communities deserve it and should demand it, but are we just going to recognize this crisis and move on without doing something about it? I hope not. This book is a call to action. Let's get started.

Acknowledgments

This work would not have been completed without the support of numerous people. First, I would like to thank the school districts who graciously opened their schools and districts to me. I especially want to thank Michelle Ed, and Dr. Errick Greene from Tulsa Public School, Mrs. Kim Huff from Hillsborough County Schools, and Roger Brossmer from Downey Unified. Additionally, I would like to thank Dr. Carey Regur for her support and guidance throughout this journey. She was especially helpful in the creation and facilitation of the nationwide principal survey. Also, thank you to Dr. Robert Cunard, colleague, and author of *The Successful Principal: Concrete Strategies and Essential Advice*, for recommending Rowman & Littlefield as a publisher for my book. Finally, I would like to thank Dr. Lawrence O. Picus of the University of Southern California who continues to mentor, encourage, and support me.

Chapter One

It's Lonely in the Middle

"The place of the principal within the school can be a very lonely one indeed."
—Walker and Qian

There is a crisis in public education that needs to be addressed immediately. This crisis is negatively impacting the performance of its students, administrators, and the longevity of site leaders. The issue is that principals are working in isolation. This isolation is leading to undermining their ability to effectively improve student achievement, make a sustained positive impact for children, and enjoy working in the profession. This phenomenon is especially relevant to site administrators because they work in an isolated environment. Specifically, principals are often the only administrators on their campus, and those who are fortunate enough to have assistant principals are still the only one holding that position at their site.

Principals are burning out and moving on at an alarming rate (Boyce & Bowers, 2016). One reason is they lack consistent and meaningful coaching. Despite research suggesting that there is a need for principal coaching and correlation to improved student performance, consistent formal support in the form of coaching is rarely seen throughout school districts nationwide. On the school campus, the principal has no one to confide in on a regular basis. Who do they go to when they need to strategize, debrief, or even vent? Typically, no one. They keep it inside and move on to the next crisis.

The main obstacle that plays a barrier is that school districts have not created a model of coaching for their principals. Today's principal is not able to truly be open to anyone on their campus about confidential issues. They have to be cognizant of who they can trust and most often this person does not exist on their campus.

As a result, this makes the position incredibly lonely. Couple this with the increased pressures and accountability administrators are facing, and the fallout is principals are abandoning the position far too early in their careers. However, this can be overcome, and this book will provide a roadmap for supporting principals.

This book will first serve as a place to acknowledge the reality that principals work in isolation, but more importantly it will be a call to action for school district decision makers to be courageous by providing their principals with coaching. The best practices uncovered in this book will help principals overcome the loneliest position in education today by making the job manageable and rewarding while focusing on the most important part of the job: improving student performance.

In between, it will uncover what the current literature has to say on the subject of principal coaching. While literature is scarce on the topic of today's principal working in isolation, what is available will provide a powerful backdrop as to why principals are leaving the position sooner than expected and how coaching is playing an important role in some school districts. Putting all of that together will draw the connection that there is a critical need to address principal isolation, but there is hope in overcoming it as well.

Moreover, in a nationwide survey, principals themselves will have a voice in this discussion (chapter 4, "What the Principals Have to Say") as they are battling in the trenches daily. They will share their experiences on the value of the coach and coachee relationship. Additionally, countless principal peers have suggested that there is great importance in writing a book on this topic as a resource for school districts to plan, design, and implement a successful coaching program. These peers not only agree with the notion that the principal works in isolation, but more importantly, they are starving for support and coaching is the vehicle to provide it.

This encouragement has provided the catalyst necessary to address the issue, bring in relevant literature, find current practical models, and implement best practices. Principals need support and in turn, the students, staff, and communities they serve will benefit from a more skilled and happy principal. By including the experiences and ideas of today's principals, the result will be the Research-Based Implementation Model (RBIM), which schools and school districts can choose from to tailor to fit the unique needs of their organization to make strides in creating a coaching model.

WHAT WILL WE LEARN HERE?

What this book will uncover through the literature is that this crisis is real. Better still, chapter 5 ("Case Studies") will offer examples of those districts already doing this work. As a result, the reader will learn hands-on, practical best practices to implement a coaching model to help principals succeed in the position and in turn get the most out of their students, teachers, and ultimately themselves.

In *School Leadership That Works* by Robert Marzano, Timothy Waters, and Brian McNulty (2005), they support this notion by suggesting, "For a school to be the launchpad to the levels of success sought by students, however, it must operate effectively" (p. 3). In order to achieve this success, it will not happen in a vacuum with principals working in isolation.

Marzano et al. (2005) continue to assert, "Whether a school operates effectively or not increases or decreases a student's chances of academic success" (p. 3). In turn, it is a moral imperative to provide our principals with support in order for them to provide the most high-quality academic experience for all children.

Furthermore, in their research, Marzano et al. (2005) encapsulate 21 Responsibilities of the School Leader, which are more than a general checklist. Their findings suggest that the highest correlation to improving student performance is Situational Awareness followed by Monitoring/Evaluating, and Resources.

They define Situational Awareness as the responsibility of being aware of the details and undercurrents of running the school and using this information to address current and potential problems. For example, principals with strong Situational Awareness are in tune with the day-to-day emotions and feelings of their schools, which helps them anticipate issues. They define Monitoring/Evaluation as the ability to monitor practices in place and their relationship to student performance, and Resources as providing "teachers with materials and professional development necessary for the successful execution of their jobs" (Marzano et al., 2005). Specifically, Monitoring/Evaluation is the feedback that principals provide teachers focused on improving student achievement.

Remember, these are only the top three of 21 Responsibilities. It is a diverse list. Clearly, principals must not only wear many hats—often on the same day—but are also expected to be proficient at all their responsibilities to ensure a safe, academically successful, and efficient school. They cannot go at it alone. It's too much. Without a doubt, this provides evidence that there is a need for coaching to help support principals in these most challenging times.

INTENDED OUTCOMES

The intended outcomes for this book are the following. First, to have an honest discussion that this is a crisis in education today, and acknowledge that the principalship is an isolated (or lonely) position and the negative impact it has on those leaders. Also, to instill a call to action for decision makers to make meaningful systemic change by implementing a coaching model in their districts for their principals.

Second, through the research conducted for this book, principals will be able to benchmark best practices of peers and aspirational organizations that are successfully implementing strategies. While comparatively few school districts nationwide have implemented a coaching model, some exemplars do exist, and this book will bring forth the lessons learned from three school districts to help the rest move forward in chapter 5, "Case Studies."

Next, with this information in hand, districts can then look inward at their own organization and begin to experiment and implement these practices to create an internal network to support principals in one of the most difficult positions in education today.

A thorough on-ground examination of best practices will be shared and some exemplars will be evaluated through a culmination of these case studies. Exemplars such as the work that is happening in Tulsa Public Schools, Downey Unified School District, and Hillsborough County Schools are three current models that will be discussed in detail.

Also, best practices may include the need for support systems such as consistent and ongoing coaching, or professional growth opportunities centering on strategies to manage the principalship for both coaches and coachees. In addition, higher education administrative credential programs will be encouraged to come alongside to partner not only to acknowledge this crisis, but also to provide additional strategies and support for overcoming this dilemma within the curriculum of their programs.

WE GET THE LONELY PART, BUT THE MIDDLE OF WHAT?

It is assumed by now that you understand why the principalship is considered lonely in nature, but what does "in the middle" refer to? Often, many who go into the career of being a principal are under the impression that upon assuming the office of the principalship one is bestowed with great powers and much autonomy. This is far from reality. Realistically, and more importantly, the reality of the principalship is that principals are middle managers, at best.

Dr. Robert Cunard, respected high school principal, colleague, and author of *The Successful Principal: Concrete Strategies and Essential Advice*, adds a historical perspective. "It used to be that principals had autonomy before accountability systems put so much pressure on school boards and district-level administrators. Once schools and districts started getting labeled as anything other than excellent, principals got squeezed," suggests Cunard.

However, that is not the perception. Most teachers, support staff, parents, and school community members see the principal as the leader of this little kingdom known as a school. Often the hierarchy of a school district, which is positioned above school sites, is not seen by these constituents, and therefore not realized.

Sure, principals make important decisions every day that impact hundreds of people. They can positively or negatively influence the climate and also shape the culture of a campus, but the principal is truly caught in the middle between the school in which they serve and the desires of those above them such as directors, assistant superintendents, superintendents, and of course the political forces that center around a school district.

Principals are reminded from time to time of their place in this hierarchy. Most often this comes during those dreaded top-down "principal's meetings." That title is a misnomer as it implies that principals somehow are running these meetings and have a voice in their agenda. However, the reality is that these meetings are a reminder that principals are to carry out the directives of others in the form of policies, procedures, programs, and desires that are created by someone other than themselves. This is not a negative, just a fact.

Principals often rely on these policies and procedures to help guide decisions. When those decisions are questioned and come under fire by a school's constituents, a principal can often truthfully state, "This is district policy." This statement may take the pressure and accountability off their shoulders.

Every school district needs clear and consistent policies; these are handed down *to* principals. Principals rarely if ever have a voice in the creation of policies or their implementation. In short, principals are caught in the middle. The sooner a principal realizes and embraces this, the better opportunity they have to successfully navigate those waters and know how far to push and when it is time to go with the agenda of others without questioning. Navigating this is a challenge and having an experienced coach to guide a principal is beneficial as this process of acceptance and understanding does not come naturally.

However, sometimes those political pressures do not come from the district level, which are also coachable moments. For example, a colleague ("Rena") shared a story of one occasion when she was a principal taking the reins at a new school site. Prior to the start of school, Rena met with her district administrative team to learn all she could about the school.

As an experienced principal, Rena knew the questions to ask to gain insight about the culture and climate of the school, but ultimately she wanted to know why she was chosen to serve there. After all, there were three principal openings and districts are typically strategic about where they place successful veteran principals. There must have been a reason why Rena was being placed at that school. She assumed the culture, climate, or political challenges would be areas that she would be expected to improve.

While the team spent most of the conversation pointing out the positives of Rena's new assignment, she could sense there was a political undercurrent in play that she was expected to be aware of and navigate through. Not a problem, she thought. "Been there, done that." Well, not exactly.

Every school is unique, and Rena soon discovered the unique features of this one as well. She learned that her predecessor was more or less asked to move on to another district. Just prior to the first day of school as she was meeting her new staff and teachers, other staff members were stopping by her office during the end of the summer vacation to introduce themselves.

One particular veteran teacher came by, and was quick to mention in her introduction, "I am a friend of a board member." Clearly, this was a message, or some would argue an underlying threat, being sent to Rena that regardless of her goals and objectives, this veteran teacher was more connected than Rena was. Not surprisingly, as time marched on, this teacher played the "friend of a board member" card even though it appeared they worked well together through many challenging issues.

Another teacher had a similar relationship with *another* board member (same school, two board members). That is pressure. Early in the school year, this particular teacher became unhappy with a decision Rena made and went directly to the board member who in turn went to the superintendent.

Thankfully, the superintendent stood by Rena's decision, but that was all. She did not offer Rena much in terms of advice and zero coaching. In short, the message was sent. Rena was caught in the middle, alone to solve this challenge, and somewhat powerless to a degree even though she had served as a principal for a number of years prior. It would have been appreciated to have a coach help her through these new challenges, someone from outside the organization whom she could confide in.

What all of this is leading up to is that the principalship is middle management and principals need regularly scheduled, on-site coaching. This book provides principals support in steering their schools through turbulent times while making a difference in the lives of students regardless of who is connected to whom. There is nothing nobler than working with children and those who do need this support.

WHY NOW?

With so many pressing needs in public education today, why should this issue be addressed now? That's a fair question, but quite simply, this work is important because principals have a tremendous responsibility as instructional leaders while ensuring a safe, nurturing, and challenging learning environment for students. Never before has the principalship been more demanding than now. Today principals are being asked to lead bigger and better to overcome issues never seen previously. For example, the recent mental health crisis is now an issue that has surfaced of late.

Coaching is critically needed because the principalship has evolved into one of the most challenging positions in public education. Prior to the late 1990s, the principalship was primarily that of a plant manager. However, due to increased accountability under federal legislation, coupled with the standards movement at the turn of the twenty-first century and societal changes, the position has evolved into the added expectation of being an instructional leader with a primary focus on teaching and learning.

Given the pressures accountability places on principals, the lessons learned here will support them in being more effective leaders. This leadership will lead to improved student performance and increased job satisfaction.

Sadly, these stressors are not often discussed nor are they a component of administrative credential program curriculum. According to Aas (2016), currently there is little known about how leadership programs can incorporate pedagogical leadership with a connection to student achievement into professional learning for would-be principals.

A report by National Policy Board for Educational Administration (NPBEA) (2002) states, "Every educational reform report of the last decade concludes that the United States cannot have excellent schools without excellent leaders. A key leverage point for meeting major challenges facing the nation's schools, therefore, is effective leadership" (p. 2). In short, Tucker, Young, and Koschoreck (2012) offer that improving leadership preparation is an important reform strategy for school improvement and increased student achievement.

As a result, once on the job, new principals are not prepared for some of these challenges. Sometimes these create a feeling in principals that they may have made a mistake in choosing to go into administration. For new hires, they leap into the position with enthusiasm and a positive spirit, but often find that they are alone, which is quite shocking and disheartening. These rookies are surprised because most likely they were recently teachers themselves. Teachers experience a culture of coaching and collaboration, a norm for quite some time, and now as principal they are thrown into the most difficult position of their career facing issues such as angry parents, student discipline, and managing a staff of adults, who are new to them, alone.

The reality is that the principal is on their own to overcome the daily obstacles of the job. Principals are preparing for an ever-changing school setting landscape, and the requirements to be successful in the position are constantly increasing in complexity. It is too challenging of a position to tackle alone and the need of support networks through coaching is a must for principals of the twenty-first century. It should no longer be optional or unusual for a principal to have a coach.

Often, school districts do not provide support programs for principals. Regularly, new hires are thrown into the job without training or professional development to prepare them for the job. How unfortunate is that? These professionals earn a credential and earn a master's degree in a challenging administrative program only to find themselves cut loose once they have accepted the job. How are they to stay current, and who can they lean on in difficult times or unknown situations? The running joke among school secretaries is that *they* train and support new principals—but that appears to be true and must change!

For veteran principals, they are being saddled with expectations that are becoming increasingly demanding such as overseeing school safety, being an instructional leader focused on student performance, and managing complex school communities, and they are moving on from the principalship as well because they realize that they do not want to sign up for more being added to their plate without support. In sum, both new hires and experienced principals require ongoing support through coaching.

Teachers are expected to be lifelong learners through internal and external professional development and embrace the ever-changing landscape of public education. However, this expectation is lacking for site leaders. Sadly, principals often learn this unfortunate reality when it is too late—when they are already in the position and it's not their fault. Without the proper guidance or training the result can be devastating as isolation often leads to making mistakes. Making decisions in a vacuum is rarely a good strategy. Principals, in turn, feel alone, unsupported, and dissatisfied with the position they worked so hard to achieve. It is no surprise that this lack of offering principals support is one of the contributing factors of principal burnout.

INTENDED READERS

Certainly, the main audience for this book is school district decision makers such as those who hire, supervise, and support principals. Specifically, superintendents, assistant superintendents, directors, and members of boards of education are considered an audience as they have the responsibility to influence, increase efficiency, and retain effective leaders by creating a culture of coaching. The relevance, research, and the hands-on advice offered here will directly impact their principals and in turn, increase student achievement.

If principals are better at performing their jobs would it not make sense that teachers would be better supported and in turn see an increase in the performance of their students? Of course principals are an important audience for this book because it is truly all about them and offering support.

Additionally, assistant principals who aspire to holding a principalship one day will also benefit from this work. Another audience would be graduate-level students who are currently in an administrative credentialing program. This content is unique and currently not addressed in these programs. In short, this is an excellent textbook to accompany administrative leadership courses.

Uniquely, the primary content of this book is aimed at the building (principal) level, with clear application to classroom and system levels as well. For example, when districts successfully implement the best practices and strategies in this book, principals will be able to spend more time in the classroom to support teaching and learning. As a result, the content will help them become more effective in their day-to-day position. Finally, on a systematic or district level, the content will benefit the organization and challenge it to look deeper into how it supports its principals to help improve their practice.

Chapter Two

An Uncomfortable Reality —Now What?

> *"Where there is failure, inadequate leadership is often a major contributory factor. Given the importance of educational leadership, the development of effective leaders should not be left to chance. It should be a deliberate process designed to produce."*
>
> —Tony Bush

Why would one suggest that the reality of principals working in isolation is uncomfortable? Why not simply a challenge? An issue? Because when organizations—especially those rich with human capital—are confronted with something so obvious (but equally significant), it leads to a feeling of discomfort because people come with strong emotions and opinions when it comes to change. While principals are craving the opportunity to be coached (more on this in chapter 4, "What the Principals Have to Say"), there are others who are "higher up" who are less sold on the notion because this is a change to the status quo.

Additionally, it is uncomfortable because now that we have acknowledged this truth, there is a call to action for decision makers to do something about it. It is incumbent upon those leading school districts to address this reality—immediately. It can no longer be ignored.

Superintendents, assistant superintendents, directors, and the like now have the responsibility to overcome this dilemma through systematic change to help support their principals. Until that occurs, however, the principal will be forced to work in isolation, which as stated prior, has dangerous implications. The crisis is real. The best and brightest principals are leaving the profession and this needs to end. Our students deserve better.

Recall that the purpose of this book is to not only support the notion that the principalship is lonely and coaching is the answer, but equally as important, to serve as a conduit to provide models for implementing a coaching model. The intent is not to scare current or future principals away from the position. In fact, the goal is quite the opposite. The purpose is to counsel them *into* it and if you are in it, to stay in it if your organization embraces and implements a true supportive coaching model (see chapter 5, "Case Studies" and chapter 6, "Best Practices, Proven Results, and Next Steps").

However, the current reality in most school districts is that this model of support is nonexistent. Unfortunately, the age-old hierarchy of how school districts are run and organized often undermines progress.

Again, this is one of those concepts not taught in graduate school. Principals often cannot recall a unit or course of study on the stark realities of the job they were so desperately excited to land. Regardless, current and future administrators need to be aware of it and help become an advocate for their own needs as professionals. Unfortunately, principals rarely act as their own advocates because they are taught to make do with less and press onward. Education needs well-trained, passionate, and professional site leaders and it needs them at their best.

TIMES, THEY ARE A-CHANGING

The current generation of principals is facing a job that looks strikingly different than those who came before them. This is not your father's principalship or even the principal many grew up with as students. The position is no longer about managing (safety, discipline, staff evaluation, etc.). It is about leading.

Today's principals often find themselves juggling competing tasks on a day-to-day basis as a result of stressors in attempts to satisfy demands from both internal and external stakeholders of their school communities. Not to mention the accountability mandates from the federal and state levels being placed on principals every day.

While those aspects of the past job description still exist, the larger focus is on being an instructional leader. As Zepeda (2014) suggests in her book, *The Principal as Instructional Leader: A Handbook for Supervisors*, while the principalship is faced with pressures and uncertainties, the position is shifting to one that is more results oriented. Zepeda (2014) asserts it is difficult to define instructional leadership, but it does include a focus on instruction with a strong dedication to student learning.

Leadership today should be about working together, not alone, grappling with the challenges that are brought forward daily. There are numerous barriers that impede being an instructional leader, such as discipline, paperwork, dealing with angry parents, managing a safe school environment, state testing, increasing special education rules and regulations, budget, community outreach, and the list goes on (Zepeda, 2014). These derail the focus on the important work that principals should be dedicated to: teaching and learning. As Covey (1995) famously wrote in *First Things First*, "The main thing is to keep the main thing the main thing," and teaching and learning should be the main thing for principals. Easier said than done in the daily life of a principal, but nonetheless it should be the goal.

Northouse (2007) takes it a step further when he addressed attributes of a negative leader. One of the most undesirable attributes he found in his research was that of *loner*. If this is true, why then do most principals work in isolation when it is acknowledged to be unhealthy? They crave support, but currently many serve in the position alone. How many principals would have signed up for this career if they knew up front that they would receive virtually no support, even less coaching, and serve in virtual seclusion? Not many.

Successful leadership, and the skill set to be an effective leader, cannot be developed in isolation. It is like expecting a basketball player to become an improved shooter by simply standing at the free-throw line, in an empty gym, with no coaching or support, trying to perfect their technique and successful shooting by attempting shot after shot without changing anything. Most likely the result would only solidify poor technique and bad practice. Doing the same thing over and over again and expecting different results is not an effective strategy. (In fact, Albert Einstein is broadly credited with exclaiming, "The definition of insanity is doing the same thing over and over again, but expecting different results.") As Sousa (2016) asserts, practice makes things permanent, not perfect.

WHOM TO CONFIDE IN?

In times of struggle, and when isolated, who can a principal confide in? Who can they reach out to? Their supervisors? Certainly not if they are new to the position for fear of showing weakness. Can a principal confide in their teachers? Absolutely not! Many issues are confidential and must be kept as such. You tell one teacher something confidential and often times the whole staff will know it by end of the lunch period. How about the classified staff? Again, no. These employees are often community members and sharing may lead to a breach of confidentiality because they are often friends and neighbors of parents.

Well, certainly principals can confide in their assistant principals, right? To a point, yes. Assistant principals more than likely may play the role of "the shoulder to cry on" versus one to truly offer suggestions and support to the sitting principal. It is not their fault; they are the folks that the principals are mentoring and they can lend an ear, but do not have experience to always provide practical solutions to the issues being faced by the principal.

Moreover, the assistant principal position is a rarity in many places (mainly in elementary schools) in part due to scarce resources as a result of the recent recession. The economic downturn was responsible for not only a decline in assistant principals, but also the fact that in numerous school districts, principals were forced to serve at multiple sites to make up for the shortfall.

The challenge is, as one superintendent said about the principalship, is that they "lead on an island." Sometimes principals just need to unload the proverbial, "Guess what happened to me today?" Or they often need support with a challenging parent or student situation. But who can they turn to without risking the story coming back to them? Letting the staff know their challenges, struggles, or worse, their areas of inexperience, may appear as incompetence. Principals are reticent to risk that. The result is often principals keeping these issues to themselves and moving on to the next crisis. Without coaching, finding that trusting relationship is nearly impossible for today's principal.

In sum, as one principal said, in times of true crisis when he needs to speak confidentially, principals are often left with only being able to call each other. However, that rarely happens. Principals become too busy with the next issue. This is a common reality when site leadership works in isolation. As a result, they often lead from behind in a reactionary mode, which is typically ineffective.

Where do the opportunities come for collegial conversations about real issues principals are facing? Please do not say during principals' meetings. Those principal meetings are hardly professional development and rarely provide an opportunity for principals grappling with the problems they are facing today. These meetings are typically an information dump—procedures and policies. A far cry from what principals truly need. They are often a parade of district level administrators such as human resources, business, and technology coming to talk *to* them, not with them. There is virtually no dialogue. It more or less resembles a monologue.

Scores of hours can be saved by simply emailing the information to principals and allowing them to stay at their school sites, or better yet, collaborating around the pressing issues they are dealing with. Why not let the principals contribute to the agenda, which should include some form of support.

In short, principals rarely get anything out of these meetings professionally, just more bureaucratic work to pile on top of the stack they gave out during the last meeting. In short, a colossal waste of time and zero time of working together, supporting one another, or receiving coaching.

A CALL FOR COACHING

The answer to supporting today's principals as they navigate this difficult position is coaching. But the implementation of creating a culture of coaching is not so easy. Coaching is the answer (more on how the literature supports this assertion in chapter 3), but what exactly is coaching in this context? Coaching is defined as a confidential, professional relationship that is individualized, one-on-one, and job specific, focused on the challenges being faced by principals today in a neutral, non-evaluative, risk-free environment. The support needs to be current, relevant, timely, and focused.

The coaching relationship should facilitate developing one's leadership and expanding their knowledge. In turn, this will lead to principals meeting the needs of their students, staffs, and communities more effectively and improving their job satisfaction.

The ultimate goal of coaching should be to provide support and guidance to the principal so they may reach their potential as a leader, enjoy working in the position, be able to tackle the pressing issues of the day, and ultimately, improve student performance. Today's principals are working in isolation in a profession that demands collaboration and support from others.

Coaching is critical to build leadership skills and leadership capacity. Principals often feel they are empty vessels yearning to be filled. They crave this; more to come on this topic in chapter 4, "What the Principals Have to Say." The coaching environment needs to be a safe place where they can be open and confidential without judgment to share their struggles.

While this is a new concept for school site leadership, it has been commonplace for teachers to receive peer coaching for years. The expectation is for teachers to have this support for their job, which is constantly increasing in complexity. The organization owes it to its principals to provide the same for them now.

In supporting this notion in recent years, there has been an increase in districts allocating funds toward instructional coaches. Odden (2009) suggests the value of instructional coaches is a critical resource to improve professional development for teachers in that they provide "in-classroom coaching assistance [that] is the key to making professional work lead to change in instructional practice that produces student learning gains" (p. 64). If we agree, then why shouldn't districts have the same type of model for its principals? Thankfully, one state is realizing those new to the position of site leadership need this type of support.

In the August 1, 2016, edition of EdCal, a cover story focused on "Coaching Needed to Build Leaders" (ACSA, 2016). This brief article highlighted the need for coaches to support the state of California's new requirement that in order to earn a Clear Administrative Services Credential, coaching must be a component of that process. As a result, ACSA has created workshops to train would-be coaches to work with new administrators in learning theory, trust and rapport building, listening skills, as well as promoting reflection and growth (ACSA, 2016). These coaches are from outside the coachee's organization.

While this is a step in the right direction, it is not enough. It is encouraging to see a state take the lead on the importance of coaching and those new to administration, but principals need support *throughout* their careers, not just in the beginning.

The benefits of coaching can be career changing and help principals become the best they can be for their school communities. Those benefits may include:

- The support from a coach helps one become more accountable and therefore a better principal.
- It seems incomprehensible to be working in such isolation while being charged with the most precious commodity we have: children. As a result, coaching should be designed to provide research-based strategies, professional development, resources, and guidance for improving student performance through a structured collaborative model.
- Coaching can be transformative. It can lead to shaping the lives of students, transforming their leadership, and significantly improving schools and districts.
- From a coach's perspective, they enjoy the process because they are able to draw on their own experiences and shared knowledge to make a difference for students.
- The relationships that are built become networks of professionals focusing on a common cause.
- Simply put, through coaching, principals can pick up new ideas. This may lead to taking those ideas and strategies into their schools, implementing them, and striving to see a difference.
- The principalship can be taxing. As the year progresses, principals are often dragging, drained, depleted, and exhausted from the grueling pace that a school year can bring. They need a balance. They want to be recharged, re-fired, and renewed.
- Principals, as you will read in chapter 4, "What the Principals Have to Say," have a pressing need to be inspired and motivated. Currently, that is lacking. Coaching can provide it.
- As stated prior, it is critical to develop a relationship that is centered on trust because principals should be free to share things with their coach that they cannot share at their school sites (ACSA, 2016).

We all know learning never ends. At least, it shouldn't. In fact, most of us hold fast to the understanding that lifelong learning is essential and educators should be models of that philosophy. The pressures, or accountability, of being a learning professional should include a principal model of coaching. Without that support, the job will overwhelm and burn out those who are so desperately needed in these challenging times in education.

Chapter Three

What the Literature Says

> *"To achieve great schools, we need great leaders, and calls for improvement have raised the stakes—and responsibilities—for those who work to lead our schools toward success."*
>
> —Farley-Ripple, Raffel, and Welch

The body of research presented in this chapter supports a model of coaching for principals. Surprisingly, most of the research centers on new or novice principals. While it is important to acknowledge this focus, all principals—new and veteran alike—need coaching support.

This chapter has numerous goals. One is to see what the experts who have gone before have to contribute to the subject of coaching. Another is to analyze what that research says and to ask what it is based upon. What are the results of research studies on coaching? Also, another goal is to reveal what data can be relied upon to support the notion that principal coaching is needed.

Moreover, this chapter will answer questions such as why are principals voluntarily leaving the position? How do the experts define coaching? What does coaching look like and how much does it cost to implement a coaching model? By the end of this chapter, we will have a clear understanding of what the literature has to say on the subject of coaching principals. This material will provide the framework of the Research-Based Implementation Model (RBIM) for Principal Coaching, which is the culminating work of this book.

WHY ARE PRINCIPALS LEAVING?

A place to begin is to acknowledge that principals are voluntarily leaving the profession at alarming rates, which is a major concern. Shockingly, the Association of California School Administrators claims that the average tenure of a California principal is three years. Comparatively, a recent study by Ed Source (2015) stated that 17 percent of teachers quit the profession after five years. The quality of the principal's work is second only to the quality of teachers when determining factors that influence school improvement, particularly in high-poverty schools (Warren & Kelsen, 2013), and this turnover is negatively impacting the ability to move these schools forward and overcome numerous barriers.

School districts throughout the nation invest countless resources into the recruitment, training, and retention of principals, but as we will learn in this section, it is not enough to overcome the dilemma of principals leaving a position that they have worked so hard to earn.

Warren and Kelsen (2013) examined this question in their article titled "Leadership Coaching: Building the Capacity of Urban Principals in Underperforming Schools," which appeared in the *Journal of Urban Learning, Teaching, and Research*. They suggest that the principalship has become a less attractive career option for educators due to the increase in working conditions that have become more challenging.

For example, they assert that today's urban school principals who serve in low performing schools are especially confronted with unique challenges as they are faced with the struggle to improve student performance in difficult circumstances. Carrying the weight of the label "failing" by federal and state legislation leads to the burden of principals being scrutinized by their community (Houle, 2006), which contributes to them wanting to leave the position.

Additionally, Darling-Hammond (2010) contends that a shortage of talented principals to lead urban schools is due to the increased job stressors many urban principals face. In short, these factors have led to principal turnover reaching crisis proportions (Darling-Hammond, 2010; Mitgang, 2012).

Boyce and Bowers (2016) suggest principal turnover is a growing concern nationwide in their *Leadership and Policy in Schools* article titled "Principal Turnover: Are There Different Types of Principals Who Move From or Leave Their Schools?" The purpose of their study was to investigate the extent to which there is a general type, or in their words, a typology, of principals who leave their schools and positions.

To guide their study, Boyce and Bowers (2016) relied upon Cullen and Mazzeo's (2008) definition of principal turnover as one principal exiting a school and being replaced by a new principal; the significant problem of principal turnover has been found to negatively impact student achievement (Béteille, Kalogrides, & Loeb, 2012; Miller, 2013). One of those studies (Beteille et al., 2012) supported that socioeconomic status and student achievement are two factors that influence principal turnover.

In other words, it was found that principals were moving from assignments in which they were serving students with low socioeconomic and underperforming students to higher socioeconomic settings with higher achieving student populations.

Boyce and Bowers (2016) also cite numerous researchers who suggest that principal turnover negatively impacts teacher and staff morale, which ultimately leads to a lack of commitment within the school and therefore is a threat to school climate. This evidence supports their desire to study the typology of principals who exit their schools.

For example, they cite Battle and Gruber's (2010) study, which suggested that in the 2008–2009 school year 18 percent of principals were designated either as movers, in which they became the principal of a new school, or as leavers, which refers to them leaving the principalship altogether.

Moreover, Boyce and Bowers (2016) concurred with DeAngelis and White's (2011) contention that recently principal turnover rates have been increasing, and Weinstein, Jacobowitz, Ely, Landon, and Schwartz's (2009) assertion that some schools have as many as five principals in a ten-year period of time. DeAngelis and White's (2011) Illinois study indicated the rate of principal turnover significantly increased over a fourteen-year period.

They claim factors such as principals leaving the position for a non-principal school position; various principal factors, including their experience, age, race/ethnicity and education; along with other school-related factors of socioeconomic status of students and student achievement impacted principal turnover.

Boyce and Bowers (2016) maintain that the impact of such findings are especially alarming as there is evidence to suggest that principals require seven years or more before they are able to successfully implement change within a school. As discussed earlier, principal turnover rates are increased in schools with large minority populations (Baker, Punswick, & Belt, 2010; Béteille et al., 2012; Gates, Guarino, Santibañez, & Ghosh-Dastidar, 2004). Considering the research on the negative impacts of principal turnover, there is a call for designing interventions to improve principal retention (Branch, Hanushek, & Rivkin, 2012; Clotfelter, Ladd, Vigdor, & Wheeler, 2006). Clearly, this supports the contention that one of those so-called interventions should be principal coaching.

Fuller and Young (2009), according to Boyce and Bowers (2016), conducted one of the most recent and most robust quantitative studies, examining principal turnover in Texas using data from 1995 to 2008. Not surprisingly, their findings were congruent with other studies and suggested that almost

50 percent of newly hired principals leave within three years and 70 percent leave within five years (Fuller & Young, 2009).

Another seminal study highlighted by Boyce and Bowers (2016) was Johnson's (2005) attempt at answering the question "Why do principals quit?" in her similarly titled piece in *Principal*. Johnson (2005) aimed at understanding why seemingly successful principals left their positions. Her study identified two different types of principals who leave the profession entirely. She labeled them as "satisfied exiters" and "unsatisfied exiters."

The unsatisfied principals, according to Johnson (2005), named a variety of reasons for leaving their positions. Those included obstacles such as engaging in the stress and workload of the position, having to constantly manage politics and bureaucracy, student discipline problems, effective instructional leadership, and more. Johnson (2005) makes suggestions of interventions that might help retain unsatisfied principals such as additional administrative support. She also offers other interventions, such as working to reduce the sense of isolation that many principals report grappling with, to help retain both types of exiting principals.

This is a critical conclusion as it supports the notion that principals work in isolation and without the proposed intervention of coaching will continue to leave the profession.

In sum, it is important to separate and acknowledge the types of principals Boyce and Bowers (2016) bring forth because leaving in and of itself does not necessarily tell the whole story. We need to have an understanding of *why* they are leaving, who they are, and where they are landing. As a result, school districts should create a model of coaching designed to support principals so they stay in the position and enjoy the job.

In Farley-Ripple, Raffel, and Welch's (2012) article titled "Administrator Career Paths and Decision Processes" in the *Journal of Educational Administration*, they focused their study on how influencers such as recruiting, developing, supporting, and retaining quality leaders are vital to both local and national reform movements. Theirs was a state-wide qualitative study of school administrator career paths in Delaware with an eye on the processes and forces that shape school administrator career paths.

They found that while some career paths and decisions are self-initiated by principals, most are influenced by other factors in the system. Some of those factors can be described as recruiting/tapping, reassigning, passing over, requesting, and removing.

The principal effect on student achievement, while only second to teachers, is often overlooked (Farley-Ripple et al., 2012; Leithwood et al., 2008). Therefore, it is critical to retain effective leaders in our schools for student success (Farley-Ripple et al., 2012). They too suggest this is becoming alarming in that they quote a recent figure from a national study indicating that schools experience a new principal every three to four years, with some schools averaging 2.8 principals in ten years (Farley-Ripple et al., 2012; Seashore-Louis, Leithwood, Wahlstrom, and Anderson, 2010).

A related work also supports the idea that some intervention, perhaps coaching, should be in place to help assist principals. Crow (1992) concluded that, "except for attention to the preparation and entry of principals, little consideration has been given to the principal's career" (p. 80). Sadly, that seems to be pervasive in education today. However, based on what we have learned thus far, coaching appears to be a solution to help overcome the factors of reassigning, removing, or passing over administrators for other positions because they will receive the support they need to be successful (Farley-Ripple et al., 2012). In terms of passing over, coaching can lead to principals being more effective and therefore more highly considered candidates for district positions, not to mention improved morale does occur when school districts promote from within. It conveys the message that principals are a valued commodity in their organization.

Farley-Ripple et al. (2012) went on to state that in a few cases principals were faced with the emotional and subsequent physical toll of the position, which led to the decision to change positions but remain in education (e.g., move from principal to assistant principal or back to teaching). This could be considered a backslide that could be ameliorated through a coaching model that is designed to support principals in managing the emotional and physical barriers of the position.

The principalship is a demanding job. The position can clearly negatively impact all facets of one's personal and professional life. Farley-Ripple et al. (2012) agree, "This affective dimension of the profession becomes important in understanding the conditions under which administrators work and highlights the human side and needs of school leaders" (p. 801).

Not surprisingly, Farley-Ripple et al. (2012) found the most significant factor in terms of administrator behavior that was influential in career decision-making was working relationships. For those who have held the position of principal, it is understood that building successful relationships with all constituents within the school community is most critical in moving a school forward. It is also known that the undoing of many principals is the inability to foster relationships. Still, this is not innate to all and the interplay of relationships begs for offering the principal support in the form of a coach who has the experience of success as a principal themselves in the area of relationship building.

Moreover, Farley-Ripple et al. (2012) concur, "Administrators we spoke with often found their working relationships to be among the most beneficial aspects of their job, while also finding them at times to be the most challenging" (p. 802). Other influential factors, according to Farley-Ripple et al. (2012), leading principals to rethink this career decision include:

- Feeling frustrated by angry or indifferent parents.
- Being dismayed by conflicts with teachers and parents.
- Facing conflicts extended beyond the school to the central office and school board.
- Inherited conditions in their schools, including the difficult task of cleaning up what previous leaders had left behind.
- Working with disadvantaged populations and communities.
- A wide range of forms of support from their central office as well as varying degrees of support.
- Frustration with systems-level issues related to policy, accountability, autonomy, district support, and job security.
- Navigating the political climate.
- Poor working conditions.

These factors came from the principals themselves and are real. However, there is hope. Thankfully, coaching can help guide principals through these rough waters so they choose to stay, not leave, because ultimately they want to stay to make a positive difference in the lives of students, which is the reason many took on the position to begin with.

Farley-Ripple et al. (2012) agree in that they assert, while acknowledging the many challenges of the job, principals reported to them they enjoyed them and expressed a belief that they are in the "right line" of work. It is true that principals embrace the constant challenges—they just need support in navigating them.

PREPARATION FOR LEADERSHIP

While the notion that school site leadership impacts student performance is widely accepted, the argument is still unclear as to what type of preparation is needed to ensure successful site leadership (Bush, 2009). Researchers, including Leithwood et al. (2008), suggest that only second to the classroom teacher, school site leadership is the most important variable in improving student performance. They argue that there is not one piece of documented evidence to support an increase in pupil learning in the absence of talented leadership (Leithwood et al., 2008).

Additionally, Warren and Kelsen (2013) add that school principals impact curriculum and instruction, attitudes and teaching practices, and in turn, student achievement (Marzano, Waters, & McNulty, 2005; Mendels & Mitgang, 2013). However, what preparation will lead to having such a positive impact?

In his article in *Educational Review*, "Leadership Development and School Improvement: Contemporary Issues in Leadership Development,"

Bush (2009) unpacks the answer to that question and notes that research supports the belief that preparation that is specific in context contributes to the quality of school site leadership. Citing the work of Daresh and Male (2000), Bush (2009) makes the case that principals in the first year often experience hardship and they find the position to be a shock as they move in to the principalship. New principals find juggling the demanding nature of the job overwhelming; and without a strong preparation program the new hire may be set up for failure.

With this in mind, it is no wonder there is an increase in some districts and states on focusing their coaching efforts on new or novice principals. More on that research later in this chapter.

Hayashi (2016) in her article "Administrative Coaching Practices: Content, Personalization, and Support," looked at principals who were emailed a blind survey. Thirty participants out of 67 responded to the survey. These principals were new administrators who had either graduated or were enrolled in year two of a Clear Administrative Services Credential program (Hayashi, 2016). In California, the "Tier II" program requires candidates to participate in a two-year coaching model. The purpose of the survey was to determine the following:

- Whether the program content was comprehensive, the personalization of the program to their own district and school site needs was sufficient
- Whether they were able to establish a relationship with a coach that provided the support they felt was necessary to improve their decision-making skills and ability to resolve challenging school site issues
- Whether their employer provided sufficient resources and financial support
- The survey was intended to assess the perceptions of the participants in order to learn what new administrators are looking for in the administrative coaching process (Hayashi, 2016, p. 178).

Her conclusions from the survey feedback were valuable. Participants stated that the program content must include a relationship with the local school district so that the program participants see immediate application to their individual job circumstances. Additionally, she found the relationship between the coach and the candidate is the key to a successful program for both the provider and the candidate, so appropriate training and preparation of the coaches is an important program component. Finally, she concluded that the program must be individualized, personal, and practical (Hayashi, 2016).

INCREASING ROLE OF THE PRINCIPAL

Bush (2009) asserts there has been a paradigm shift in the expanded role of the school leader. Specifically, he cites the increasing complexity of school contexts while recognizing the need for effective pre-service program support and development for would-be leaders (Bush, 2009). In terms of the expanding role of the principalship, Bush (2009) notes that responsibilities imposed upon principals, and especially those new to the position, are increasingly being applied by those overseeing them.

Also, the accountability pressures stemming from the federal, state, and local level—including stakeholders within the school—are growing, immense, and are laid at the feet of the principal (Bush, 2009). Bush (2009) also contends that the growing trend of decentralization is leading to the expanding role of the principal, putting them in the line of fire as the face of the school.

An example from California is the shift in public school funding, which includes parents having a greater say in where funds are allocated. State legislation includes principals being expected to hold public forums, leading to challenges of how their school is governed versus the intended law's goal of being a collaborative exercise. What parents do not usually understand is the notion that the principal is truly middle management. While principals appear to the community as the place where the buck stops, there are many bureaucratic layers in the hierarchy above them in which they serve.

Additionally, Wise (2010) suggests that Heifetz and Linsky (2002) capture the essence of this dilemma best when they wrote of the difference between adaptive and technical leadership, in which today's principals (leaders) can no longer rely only upon technical expertise to solve problems, but on seeking solutions that are "adaptive because they require experiments, new discoveries, and adjustments from numerous places in the organization or community" (p. 13).

Complex is now a descriptor of the principalship. The world is becoming increasingly complex due to rapid changes of the world around us in the twenty-first century. In *The World Is Flat* (2005), Friedman introduced us to a new world order by asserting a "flattening" world mainly due to recent technological advances. Friedman (2005) defined "flat" as meaning there are no longer obstacles that prevent individuals from communicating and collaborating on a global level.

This change has been unprecedented and has not only impacted economics but education and the responsibilities of principals to keep up as well. Bush (2009) concludes that this has inevitably "led to increased accountability pressures on site-based leaders who have to deal with increasing complexity and unremitting change" (p. 377).

Crow (2006) adds to the conversation by suggesting the dynamic and complicated environment for principals includes "responding to the information needs of teachers and students, creating resources to acquire hardware and software, developing a professional learning environment to support the use of technology, and closing the digital divide between rich and poor students" (p. 315). The responsibility of preparing the students of today for the unknown world of tomorrow is a massive undertaking. Another factor, asserts Crow (2006), are the changing student demographics in schools, which is also contributing to the complexity of the principal's job.

Requirements such as curriculum standards, achievement benchmarks, programmatic requirements, advancements in technology, and other policy directives from many sources result in a need for leaders to have heightened levels of expertise (Young, Crow, Murphy, & Ogawa, 2009). Principals must also respond to increasing needs of diversity in students, such as cultural background, immigration status, income disparities, physical and mental disabilities, and variations in learning capacities (Witziers, Bosker, & Krüger, 2003). These are just a few conditions that solidify the need to investigate how schools are being led and the value coaching provides in providing the principal support.

In "Revolutionary Leadership" (*Leadership*), Bossi (2007) concurs, "the principal's role has shifted from managing and evaluating individual instructors to creating and maintaining data-driven collaborative cultures" (p. 32). While his emphasis is on a coaching model for new principals, his assertion is that today's principal (new or veteran alike) must focus upon the academic success of all students, while serving as both instructional leader and learning leader of the school (Bossi, 2007).

In short, the principalship requires a new set of skills and abilities and, "the principal must now be able to engage in systems thinking and demonstrate the ability to both understand and guide complex processes of evaluation, change, and group development" (Bossi, 2007, p. 36).

Bossi (2008), in his *Leadership* article "Does Leadership Coaching Really Work?" continues to advocate for those new to the position in that he maintains that implementing instructional programs, best teaching practices, managing the budget, and personnel issues often are barriers to success for new principals.

As Bossi (2008) contends, this could have a devastating result. He says, "It is failing to understand, respect and effectively respond to all the diverse elements of the school community . . . that can prematurely end a new principal's career" (Bossi, 2008, p. 32). To test his hypothesis that coaching new principals would see an improvement in student performance, he conducted a study using data from two cohorts (2003–2005, 2004–2006) of new principals.

From the first year of coaching to the second, 40 of 50 principals in his study saw an increase in standardized test scores by the students at their school sites. In the second year, 22 of 25 sustained the growth as well. In addition to the increase in student performance, Bossi (2008) supports the notion that when a school district chose to invest resources, "in the development of their site leaders through coaching, those site leaders stayed with the district" (p. 34). Why? The difference is with coaching, the principal is no longer making isolated decisions.

While Bossi (2008) suggests what coaching is, he is also quick to point out what is not. First, it is important to note it is neither therapy nor counseling. It is not the coach leading the principal on a leash around the campus (Bossi, 2008). In short, it is a collaborative effort. It is more than improving instruction and student achievement. The coach's role goes beyond and focuses on growth and building independence and leadership capacity within that site leader (Bossi, 2008).

Bossi (2008) sums it up like this, "Leadership coaching is certainly needed. It makes sense. It is based, philosophically, upon a model that complements, extends and applies training through intensive, site-based, individualized follow-up professional support. It works" (p. 36).

SUPPORTING LEADERSHIP THROUGH COACHING

In addition to Bossi's (2008) study, there are others who also contribute to the conversation as well. For example, Rich and Jackson (2005) studied pairing novice and experienced principals together in a coaching relationship in their piece "Peer Coaching: Principals Learning from Principals; Pairing Novice and Experienced Principals Provides Both with Opportunities to Promote Reflective Thinking in Their Decision-Making" (*Principal*).

Rich and Jackson (2005) support this model because, "given that the challenges of the principalship continue far beyond the first year or two on the job, a peer-coaching partnership provides both the novice and experienced principal an opportunity to work within a framework that supports reflection on practice, thinking, and foundational beliefs. Both principals can expect to benefit" (pp. 31–32).

Those benefits include:

- Establishing an intrinsically rewarding, professional relationship that helps to limit the feeling of isolation;
- Becoming aware of areas where a need for improvement may exist;
- Improving administrative skills by sharing successful practices and solutions;

- Learning to consider and address issues in a larger context by thinking "outside the box"; and
- Becoming generally more reflective in evaluating all events with an eye toward future improvement.

Interestingly, Rich and Jackson (2005) suggest that their coaching relationship model is not supported in numerous school districts because districts often hold supervisors accountable for training of principals when they are already overworked with obligations. As a result, principals are then left to cultivate collegial communities of professional learning (Rich & Jackson, 2005). In short, Rich and Jackson (2005) support this coaching model. "Because the principalship is an extremely rewarding but equally challenging responsibility, both novice and experienced principals must decide whether to navigate these choppy waters in isolation" (p. 33).

The work of Bloom, Castagna, Moir, and Warren (2005) contributes greatly to the body of research on the subject of supporting new and veteran principals through coaching. They assert that coaching should be a relationship built on trust and permission (Bloom et al., 2005). Additionally, Bloom et al. (2005) add the importance of the use of appropriate strategies, the need for a coach to be committed to the relationship, with the goal of providing professional, organizational, and personal support to the coachee.

Moreover, Bush, Glover, and Harris (2007) suggest coaching is most effective when there is a strategic matching of the coach and coachee. Also, the training that the coach receives must be specific and thorough (Bush et al., 2007). Additionally, leadership coaches experienced in educational administration can give their coachees, such as principals early in their careers, a direct connection to practical knowledge (Browne-Ferrigno & Muth, 2006).

Danielson and McGreal (2000) would concur and suggest coaching involves an individual with "experience, expertise, wisdom, and/or power who teaches, counsels, and helps less experienced or less knowledgeable personals develop professionally and personally" (p. 253).

A study conducted by Warren and Kelsen (2013) examined the results of leadership coaching of urban public school administrators in underperforming schools on the improvement of their knowledge, skills, and dispositions. Specifically, their study investigated student achievement growth at those schools with leadership and management of principals participating in a coaching program (Warren & Kelsen, 2013).

Their study yielded positive responses from both coaches and coachees. Principals and coaches noted high levels of change in knowledge, skills, and dispositions as a result of the coaching experience (Warren & Kelsen, 2013). Additional feedback from participants included being guided by their coach to transform the school and increased student performance by supporting them in dealing with union issues, and building relationships especially with those more difficult personalities (Warren & Kelsen, 2013). Also, participants recognized the focus on instructional strategies provided by their coach, and acknowledged growth in both professional and self-actualized reflective practice (Warren & Kelsen, 2013).

In conclusion, Warren and Kelsen (2013) maintain that "leadership coaching, though a relatively new aspect of educational administration, provides the support principals need and a structure for contextualized job training" (p. 20). Further, the job-embedded nature of the coach-principal relationship offers practical and timely opportunities for relevant learning (Fullan, 2008; Novak, Reily, & Williams, 2010; Smith, 2007; Stein & Gewirtzman, 2003).

Bloom, Castagna, and Warren (2003) in their *Leadership* article titled "More Than Mentors: Principal Coaching" claim that "there is a growing consensus that traditional pre-service programs have not adequately prepared candidates for the principalship" (p. 20). They also believe an effective principal is requirement of school improvement (Bloom et al., 2003). However, the authors suggest that there is a shortage of strong candidates for the principalship, and a concerning trend that those with relatively limited experience are moving into the position (Bloom et al., 2003).

While Bloom et al. (2003) support a coaching model, they are quick to point out that there is a distinction between coaching and mentoring. They begin by suggesting that mentors are typically peers who currently hold the same position (Bloom et al., 2003). Also, they purport that unfortunately the mentoring most principals receive has limitations such as inconsistency in reliability of delivery, as informal mentors are consumed by their own jobs (Bloom et al., 2003).

Bloom et al. (2003) argue that "the most effective coaches are generally outsiders who, while professional experts, have leadership coaching as their primary work . . . novice (and perhaps all) principals need an external coach as a source of confidential and expert support around the wide-ranging, problematic and often deeply personal issues that they must deal with from their first days on the job" (p. 22). It is important to highlight that the authors imply that experienced principals also need ongoing support and professional development through coaching, and that a coach can play a key role of that process (Education Research Services [ERS], 2000).

DEFINING COACHING

Earlier, principal coaching was defined as a confidential, professional relationship that is individualized, one-on-one, and job specific focused on the challenges being faced by principals today in a neutral, non-evaluative, risk-free environment. The support needs to be current, relevant, timely, and focused. This relationship should facilitate developing one's leadership and expanding their knowledge. In turn, this will lead to principals meeting the needs of their students, staffs, and communities more effectively. In this section we will see how others define coaching leadership.

In the New Teacher Center's *Coaching Leaders to Attain Student Success*, Hargrove (2008) says that coaching requires the coach to "see what others may not see through the high quality of his or her attention or listening; [be] in the position to step back from the situation so that they have enough distance from it to get some perspective; help people see the difference between their intentions and their thinking or actions; and help people cut through patterns of self-deception caused by defensive thinking and behavior" (New Teacher Center, 2008, p. 1). Hargrove (2008) continues to describe coaching as a way to "help people achieve something seemingly impossible and make a difference in their world" by pushing them toward extraordinary results, and strongly argues that coaching is "the fastest, most powerful way to develop leaders" (Hargrove, 2008, pp. x–xi).

Lochmiller (2014), when studying an induction program for principals, also suggested that a coaching model is one of a "learning relationship" (Rhodes, 2012, p. 246) between two parties. That coaching relationship helps the coachee clarify and address their professional or personal goals (Lochmiller, 2014; Bloom et al., 2005).

Lochmiller (2014) emphasizes that "effective coaching requires careful recruitment and selection of coaches, training and ongoing support of coaches in effective coaching methods, clarity of purpose about the client's goals for the coaching activity, accountability and feedback to improve the coaches' practice, and high levels of confidentiality and trust between the coach and client" (Bloom et al., 2005; Killion, 2012; Killion & Harrison, 2006; p. 63).

Providing a robust definition of leadership coaching, Bossi (2008) contends it is "an individualized, situational, goal-oriented, professional relationship focused upon the development of leadership which takes into account the circumstances and the most essential challenges of today and develops the ability of the coachee to successfully master the challenges of tomorrow" (p. 34).

Additionally, Bloom et al. (2003) validate researchers' definition by adding what coaching is not. They offer, "It is important to understand that coaching is not training . . . it is the coachee who determines the focus of the coaching session. We should also be careful not to confuse coaching with therapy. Coaching focuses upon goal accomplishment" (pp. 23–24).

WHAT DOES COACHING LOOK LIKE?

Now that you have a fairly consistent definition and conceptual framework of what coaching is, or is not, the question then becomes, what does coaching look like? For example, who is being coached, how they are being coached, what is the setting, the frequency, and so on. These questions and others will be addressed in this section as numerous researchers weigh in on this topic and their findings are worthy of note.

Wise (2010), whose article, appropriately titled "School Leadership Coaching: What Does it Look Like?" begins by sharing a quote from a second-year elementary school principal reflecting on her coaching experience: "Having the opportunity to collaborate and share ideas and experiences has had the greatest effect because principals do not have the opportunity to share and reflect with each other" (p. 1).

Moreover, Wise (2010) argues that it (the principalship) is becoming increasingly evident that principals are no longer able to rely on previous styles and models of leadership or management to adapt to situations that are unique and have never been seen previously in the principalship. In short, Wise (2010) says, "Simply stated, in the dynamics of rapid educational change, principals are often not prepared for the multiple and dynamic issues that they face. With these challenges, principals need support to be successful" (p. 2).

As a result of these challenges, Wise (2010) sought to answer the research question, "What does principal coaching look like?" There were a total of ninety-four responses who provided the background on what coaching looks like in their experiences. The breakdown of the respondents was as follows:

- 63.8 percent (60) were female
- 36.2 percent (34) were male
- The average age was 47.0 years
- The average service time in their current position was 4.5 years
- 83 percent (78) were principals
- 10.6 percent (10) were serving as vice principals
- 6.4 percent (6) held other positions of leadership
- The respondents represented a total of 89 schools in 51 school districts throughout California
- Respondents working in elementary schools: 61.7 percent (58)
- K–8 schools: 2.1 percent (2)
- Middle/intermediate schools: 13.8 percent (13)
- High schools: 17.0 percent (16)
- District or county office: 5.3 percent (5)
- Respondents indicated an average of 1.7 years of receiving coaching (p. 2)

Wise (2010) described the frequency of the coaching sessions as varying, with one-half of the respondents specifying that coaching sessions took place on average twice per month, while nearly 30 percent indicated that the sessions took place one time per week. Finally, just under 20 percent indicated that their coaching sessions took place once a month or less. Additionally, Wise's (2010) study indicated that almost all respondents said that their coaching sessions took place on their site and 75 percent of those sessions lasted from one to two hours in length (p. 2).

Finally, Wise (2010) went one step further in that the respondents were asked to provide a general picture of what the discussions with their coach centered upon. Those included:

- Establishing the guideline that their conversations were confidential
- A debrief of current issues and events
- Goal setting
- A focus on best practices
- Words of encouragement and inspiration

All of these were driven by a trusting relationship, probing questions, and a push by the coach to move the coachee to take on situations with a difference approach (Wise, 2010).

Bloom et al. (2003) claim "that effective coaches move between instructional coaching strategies, in which the coach serves as expert consultant, collaborator and teacher; and facilitative strategies, in which the coach adopts a mediational stance, with a primary focus upon building the coachee's capacity through metacognition and reflection" (p. 24). As a result, their professional development program, Coaching Leaders to Attain Student Success (CLASS), centers on building their support through goal setting, self-reflection, and problem solving.

Aas and Vavik (2015) support the coaching of school leaders as it has become a method of helping them understand and handle their complex jobs. They contend that "coaching is a bridge between general theory-driven basic competences and the personal and situated practice in which the realities of leadership are encountered" (Aas & Vavik, 2015, p. 252).

They present a different approach of coaching (group-coaching), which is a more recent leadership coaching model in a pre-service program in Oslo (Aas & Vavik, 2015). In contrast to one-on-one coaching, coaching in a group setting consists of six coachees supported by one coach (Aas & Vavik, 2015). All coachees participate in each session taking turns sharing reflections and asking questions (Aas & Vavik, 2015).

Bickman, Goldring, De Andrade, Breda, and Goff (2012) suggest that coaching for school principals "is becoming a more popular approach to leadership development" (Bickman et al., 2012, p. 2).

Bickman et al. (2012) provided yet another model of leadership coaching in their article titled "Improving Principal Leadership Through Feedback and Coaching." The purpose of their study was to evaluate the effectiveness of fast-growing executive coaching strategy utilizing a feedback and coaching intervention in which the primary focus was to improve the quality of principal leadership (Bickman et al., 2012). They implemented their study in a large urban school district located in the southeastern part of the United States. Of the eligible 108 principals, 76 consented to participate and were then randomly assigned to the treatment or control groups (Bickman et al., 2012).

In part one of the study, the feedback principals received was provided by teachers on the principal's instructional leadership, and the teachers' trust of them (Bickman et al., 2012). Additionally, principals conducted a self-rating and in turn compared the teacher feedback to their own ratings (Bickman et al., 2012). In the second part of the study, the principals worked with trained coaches on how to use and integrate that information into their educational practice.

Demographics of the study included:

- 76 principal participants
- 2.4 principal average years in their current position
- 5.6 principal average years of service in the school district
- 1.6 teacher average years at their school
- 1.1 teacher average years with their principal

Their belief was that "feedback alone, without supports for implementing the feedback, may fail to improve leadership" (Bickman et al., 2012, p. 2). As a result, they predicted that their intervention would improve principals' leadership and trust, and, ultimately, enhance student achievement. Their coaching model included:

- 15 sessions per school year
- Coaches scheduled sessions with their principals
- Sessions typically were held in the principal's office
- Meetings lasted between 45 and 90 minutes
- A specific protocol or procedures were not utilized
- Meeting reminders were automated and emailed to both coaches and principals
- The content focused on developing principals' knowledge and skills in the service of developing instructional leadership behaviors and achieving outcomes (Bickman et al., 2012)

Bickman et al. (2012) concluded that when coaching and feedback are combined, the effects are much more significant and greatly depend on the principal's perception of the validity of the teachers' feedback coupled with the number of coaching sessions attended. They claim that their "study provides new experimental evidence of the efficacy of feedback and coaching as a program for leadership change and development aimed at improving instructional leadership and teacher principal trust" (Bickman et al., 2012, p. 4).

In sum, they assert that this is achieved by building an evolving relationship, goal setting, questioning, listening, assessing, providing feedback, confronting, motivating, action planning, establishing accountability, and in the end supporting (Bickman et al., 2012).

In their article "Implementation of a Coaching Program for School Principals: Evaluating Coaches' Strategies and the Results," Huff, Preston, and Goldring (2013) presented a multi-phase coaching model that was designed to help principals improve their instructional leadership practices. They define coaching "as a helping relationship between (1) a client with managerial authority in an organization, and (2) a consultant who uses a wide variety of behavioral techniques and methods to help the client achieve a mutually identified set of goals, within a formally defined cooperative agreement" (Huff, Preston, & Goldring, 2013, p. 507). In this relationship, a coach facilitates a client's active engagement, learning and commitment to a course of action (Bacon & Spear, 2003).

Huff et al. (2013) developed a five-phase model of coaching to capture the key paths that principals follow with their coaches to understand feedback and make meaningful changes in their leadership practices (Mavrogordato & Cannon, 2009). The basic phases in their model are:

1. Groundwork (building an effective working relationship)
2. Assessment and feedback
3. Goal setting
4. Action planning
5. Ongoing assessment and support

The authors make a case for their model, and the need for coaching, based on research that supports new strategies to train both new and experienced administrators (Huff et al., 2013). They offer, "Despite this recent interest in coaching as a strategy for leadership development for school principals, little research has examined these coaching strategies and their impacts" (p. 504).

James-Ward (2011), in her article titled "The Development of an Infrastructure for a Model of Coaching Principals," studied a district leadership program that specifically focused on the creation of a coaching program for elementary principals. She asserts that the need for support and principal training has never been more important than it is today (James-Ward, 2011).

James-Ward (2011) concurs with other researchers. She argues, "Today, the job of the principal has changed from one of site manager to that of an all-encompassing school leader. Principals are expected to exhibit leadership and have knowledge of curriculum design and instructional strategies. They are expected to evaluate and refine curricular practices to ensure effective execution of programs, models, and pedagogy" (James-Ward, 2011, p. 2). Also, she validates the notion that principals are facing demanding federal mandates, which comes with it considerable pressure (James-Ward, 2011).

She also makes a case for both new and experienced principals benefitting from leadership coaching as a means to navigate a challenging, high-demanding, and multifaceted environment.

James-Ward (2011) suggests that coaching offers a continuous learning process. She believes, "Coaching offers school leaders opportunities to learn and improve their craft by building a trusting relationship and using collaboration, instruction, facilitation, reflection, and transformational strategies" (James-Ward, 2011, p. 3).

Her study focused on sixteen principals in a model that included:

- A personal coach for each principal
- The goal was to improve teaching and thus student performance
- Monthly meetings were held between coaches and district administration
- Coaches and principals met one or two times weekly for a six-month period
- District leaders recommended former administrators with track records of significantly improving student achievement to serve as coaches.
- Eight coaches were selected from that list
- All of the coaches were former principals
- The eight coaches also met by themselves once a month to collaborate, confidentially discuss issues related to their coaching relationship, discuss professional readings, and share coaching strategies (James-Ward, 2011, p. 4)

While James-Ward (2011) acknowledges that school district, national principal organizations, and state departments of education acknowledge the importance of leadership coaching (Bloom et al., 2003; Fink & Resnik, 2001; Stickel, 2005), "there is little or no evidence from the research about districts creating systems to regularly communicate with leadership coaches or on developing learning communities for their coaches" (p. 8). The district in her study did just that in developing an effective leadership coaching infrastructure as a professional learning community (James-Ward, 2011).

WHAT DOES COACHING SOUND LIKE?

Now that we have an idea about the value of coaching, the need for it, and what it looks like, one question may linger: What does the literature say coaching sounds like? If we sat in on a coaching session, what might the words be—the questions? How far does one dig? What strategies would an expert coach incorporate to provide meaningful support to the coachee? As we will see in this section, a successful coaching relationship is far more than simply scheduling a time to "talk shop"; there needs to be some clearly defined strategies involved.

Undoubtedly, the research we have learned thus far makes a case for reflective thinking as a component to effective coaching. Rich and Jackson (2005) provide the following questions as parting points for reflective thinking in a coaching model:

- "How would you describe . . . ?"
- "Can you recall what occurred . . . ?"
- "What happened when you . . . ?"
- "What are you hoping to accomplish by . . . ?"
- "What reasons guided your choice of . . . ?" (p. 33)

Bloom et al. (2005) take it further by stating, "Powerful coaching is grounded in the basic skills of listening, observing, and questioning" (p. 33). They assert that a successful coach can accomplish this by focusing on the coachee's facial expressions, gestures, words, and vocal inflections coupled with their own reactions to the coachee.

COACHING FOR EXPERIENCED PRINCIPALS

Smith (2007), in *Mentoring for Experienced School Principals: Professional Learning in a Safe Place*, suggests that in recent years mentoring of school principals has become increasingly popular and particularly so in the area of leadership development. In this case, her definition of mentoring is interchangeable with coaching. Her study focused on the mentoring of experienced elementary principals in Auckland, New Zealand, because in her experience, it is less prevalent compared to the mentoring of those new to the position (Smith, 2007).

Additionally, her research yielded feedback from the principals studied who identified a number of elements of her mentoring process as being valuable (Smith, 2007). Smith (2007) concluded that the results of her study helped in the development of a model of peer mentoring for experienced principals that was based on the idea of communities of practice. In short, hers was a group approach to the process of mentoring versus a model of one-on-one coaching. The group setting is not optimal as it does not provide the most risk-free and private environment.

Smith (2007) cites others who define a mentor as one who offers support, guidance, and advice in order to facilitate personal and career development (Kram, 1988; Carruthers, 1993; Bell, 2000; Roberts, 2000). Moreover, Smith (2007) asserts that the coach and coachee relationship is when "the mentor assists the mentee in 'a process that is about enabling and supporting—sometimes triggering—major change in people's life and work. As such it is about developing the whole person, rather than training in particular skills'" (Clutterbuck & Megginson, 1999, p. 3).

Additionally, Smith (2007) cites the work of Clutterbuck and Megginson (1999) to support the notion that the coaching interaction is often hierarchical, with the entities differing in experience in terms of their professional standing, status, knowledge, and power, but is not always the case. Fritts (1998) agrees and argues to support peer coaching in that "mentors in modern organizations are increasingly likely to be equal in status to the mentees" (p. 3).

Like others, Smith (2007) also asserts that the mentoring of principals has been mostly dedicated to new principals while these opportunities for experienced principals are rarely mentioned in the literature. However, Smith (2007) cites the work of Crow and Matthews (1998) to define that "midstage" (experienced) principal as those who have the perception that they have mastered the skills, knowledge, values, and behaviors of the principalship. Smith (2007) makes the case for the need for coaching of experienced principals in that "professionals in mid-career tend to operate alone; they do not always allocate time to reflect on their own practice and gather appropriate feedback from others. They are also inclined to seek out others like themselves with whom to share the mentoring journey and thus form peer mentor relationships within a group of colleagues" (p. 279).

Especially, Smith (2007) lists support, sharing of ideas, problem solving, improved confidence, professional development, empathy, and counseling as positive outcomes for principal coachees (Hansford & Ehrich, 2005).

WHAT WOULD IT COST?

Lochmiller (2014) conducted a cost feasibility study estimating the cost of providing leadership coaching to every new principal hired in the state of Washington. His estimate was based on the cost to compensate principal coaches in both secondary and elementary schools. He argues that while there is a wealth of research on professional development aimed at teachers, there is little on professional development for school site administrators (Lochmiller, 2014).

He based his study on the premise that policymakers are faced with the issue of funding leadership coaching, which is a successful component of administrator professional development (Lochmiller, 2014). Lochmiller (2014) asserts that policymakers often perceive there is an excessive cost to implementing such a program and as a result they are reluctant to deliver this needed support. This is also an impediment to implementing a large-scale (i.e., statewide) coaching program for site administrators (Lochmiller, 2014). However, Lochmiller (2014) suggests that these assumptions may be inaccurate or not based on research.

His analysis led him to suggest that such a model would cost between $4.01 and $12.35 based on a per pupil allocation (Lochmiller, 2014). He argues that these costs may vary depending on the selected program model, state context, and coaching fees incurred (Lochmiller, 2014).

Lochmiller (2014) cites the work of Villani (2005), who focused on mentoring and induction programs for new principals. His cost analysis led her to suggest that if an organization undertook such a program, the cost would range from $30,000 to $800,000 for a program in which 25–125 principals would participate annually (Vilanni, 2006). While Lochmiller (2014) offers that the increasing body of research suggests that principals have a positive effect on student learning, the fiscal realities of state education budgets have yet to catch up and run counter to that evidence (Hallinger & Heck, 1996, 2009; Hallinger, 2011; Leithwood & Louis, 2012), and could also greatly benefit from the implementation of a coaching program (Daresh, 2004).

Lochmiller (2014) cites data from the International Coaching Federation that within the business field, there may be as many as forty thousand leadership coaches throughout the world, which could generate up to $2 billion in revenue annually. This raises the question, why does the business sector not only understand the value of coaching, but also clearly implement it, while in education circles research has supported leadership coaching for over a decade but it is still scarce? Because public education often relies on old hierarchal structures and launching such a coaching program would need to come from the top-level management within the organization.

Moreover, Lochmiller (2014) claims, "While the development of statewide coaching programs may be viable financially, their development does raise significant new questions and potential policy challenges" (p. 12). The results of his analysis provide compelling evidence for policymakers to consider expanding coaching for school administrators as a professional development strategy (Lochmiller, 2014) possibly as a statewide initiative.

Bossi (2008) focused his two-year coaching model on new principals, which he suggests would cost $7,500 ($3,750 per) for each principal. Keep in mind, his research is roughly ten years old so inflation and added costs should be considered. He asserts it makes sense for superintendents to make the investment "in the success and development of a principal in whom the district is investing well over $200,000 (two years salary/benefits)" (Bossi, 2008, p 36). Bossi (2008) stresses that the recruitment, which includes, advertising, paper-screening, interviewing, checking references, is likely to cost between $5,000 and $10,000.

CONCLUSION

Bloom et al. (2003) suggest that coaching does make a difference and, "is a worthwhile investment. It is not surprising that principals who receive coaching say they appreciate the support and that it has made a positive difference for them . . . they are more engaged in instructional leadership, they actually are spending more time on instructional issues and are addressing them with more skill" (p. 27).

Lochmiller (2013) conducted a three-year study for an induction program for new administrators and concurs that coaching works. While this did not include the recommendation of involving novice and experienced principals, his findings support the notion that coaching matters. He focused those findings from the coach's perspective and responsibilities in that the data he collected suggested what would be most effective:

- Coaches should adopt different strategies to support the principal in each year of their work. They should be maintaining a broad focus on issues related to instructional leadership
- Strategies used by the coach depend on the nature of the issues being discussed
- The confidence of principal as an administrator should also be a focus
- The coach's perception that the staff was ready to address challenges related to teaching and learning
- Coaches used instructional coaching strategies to build the administrator's confidence throughout the first year of their work with the novice administrators (p. 70)

In short, the literature in this chapter clearly supports the case for coaching today's principals. With the added stressors of the position forcing principals to exit the job, and the impact it has on those considering it, the time is now to make coaching principals a priority.

Chapter Four

What the Principals Have to Say

"If you have an opportunity to use your voice you should use it."
—Samuel L. Jackson

The purpose of conducting this research was to provide an avenue for principals to have a voice on the subject of principal coaching. A secondary purpose was to learn what aspects of the coaching relationship worked, and also what could have made the experience more effective. Initially, knowing that the typical completion rate for surveys is around 1 percent, the goal was to obtain at least 150 responses. However, an astonishing 836 administrators completed the survey, which was an unexpected surprise and indicates that there is great passion for the topic of principal coaching.

METHODOLOGY

In 2017, a survey was sent electronically to administrators throughout the United States in California, Washington, New York, Maine, South Carolina, Ohio, Nebraska, Rhode Island, Arkansas, North Dakota, and New Jersey. The survey was sent to 13,671 collected email addresses of U.S. administrators. Returned email addresses that were obsolete totaled 6.0 percent, or 820. Those who responded to the survey totaled 836, an impressive rate of 6.1 percent. It can be assumed that administrators who had no experience with coaching might have had no reason to complete the survey, which perhaps makes the return rate even more notable.

The subjects were surveyed to determine if the administrators had experience as either a coach or coachee and if so, what the strengths of the program were. Conversely, participants were also asked what could have made the coaching relationship stronger. Finally, the survey asked respondents who both had and did not have coaching experience if they thought a coaching model would be valuable. The survey was intended to gather qualitative data from administrators on their experiences and perceptions of the coaching relationship. The data was collected using an online survey provider.

SURVEY RESULTS

Figures 4.1 through 4.7 portray the demographics of the survey participants. The respondents were each asked to provide their age and the geographic area in which they reside. Additionally, respondents were asked the number of years they have served in school administration, current administrative assignment, if they had ever participated in a coaching relationship, if the coaching relationship was effective, and how valuable would it be for them to have a confidential coach.

In addition, two constructed response, or open-ended, questions were asked. For those who answered "yes" to having participated in a coaching relationship, they were asked, what aspects of the coaching relationship made it effective? Also, those same respondents were asked, what would have made the experience more effective?

The majority of subjects (33.17 percent) were participants from the western United States. However, overall, the sample included a fairly balanced

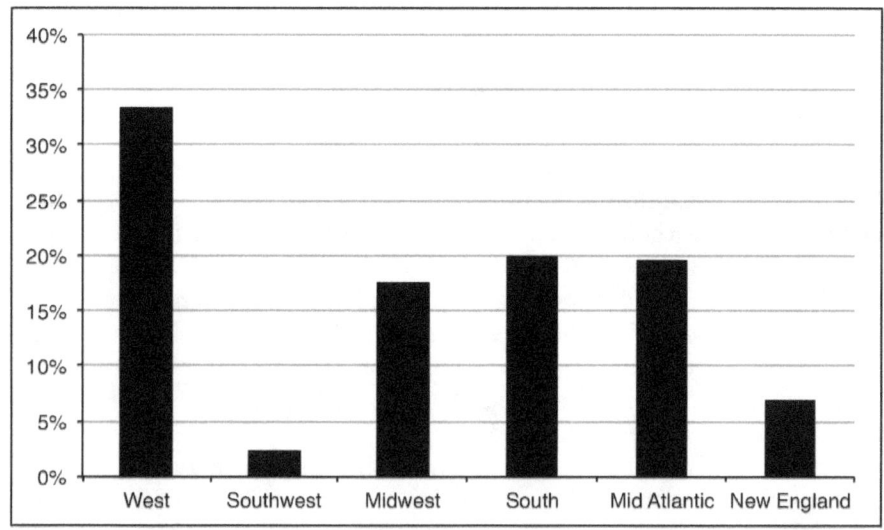

Figure 4.1. U.S. Geographic Area of Respondents.

representation from all geographic areas of the country. Two respondents chose not to answer this question.

Of the 836 subjects, over 24.25 percent were between the ages of thirty-five to forty-four, with the higher percentage at 42.34 percent in the forty-five to fifty-four age range. Two respondents chose not to answer this question.

Most of the respondents have served as administrators for eleven or more years, which is indicative of veteran principals who later overwhelmingly stated that coaching is valuable. Clearly, if experienced principals endorse something, you know it is of value. Two respondents chose not to answer this question.

The level of current assignment varied with the majority in serving in elementary education at 44.22 percent, followed by 23.25 percent in high school, then middle school with 14.34 percent, only 1.08 percent in preschool, and the other 16.99 percent representing administrators in other positions. Looking deeper, those administrators who answered "other" consisted of a number of administrative positions including:

- Superintendent (36 responses)
- Superintendent/Principal (4)
- District Level Director (20)
- Kindergarten–1st Grade (1)
- Transitional Kindergarten–8th Grade (8)

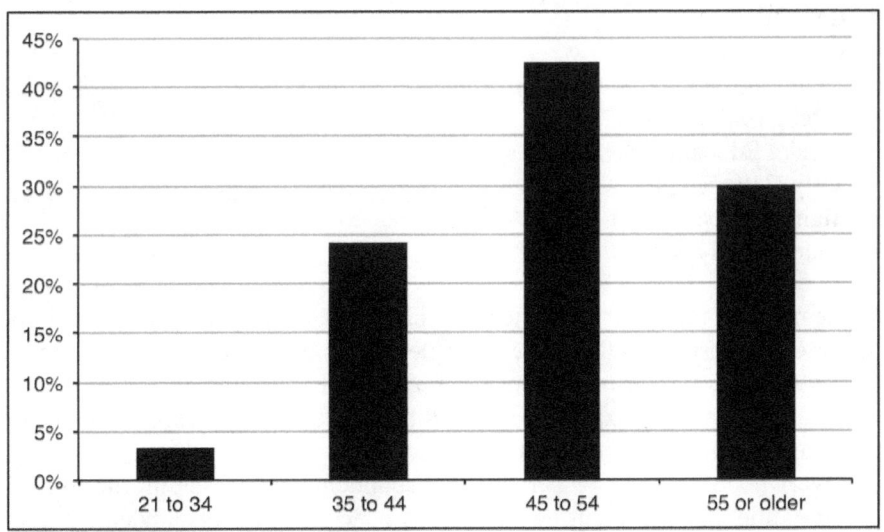

Figure 4.2.   Age Range of Respondents.

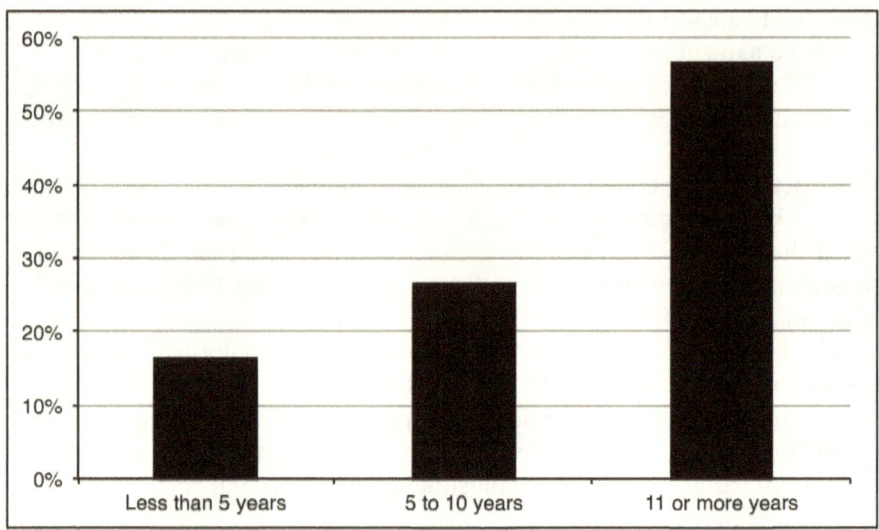

Figure 4.3. Years in Administration.

- Pre-K–12th (12)
- Kindergarten–12th Grade (14)
- Kindergarten–8th Grade (23)
- 3rd–9th Grade (1)
- 6th–12th Grade (5)
- 7th–12th Grade (3)
- Middle School (1)
- Continuation High School (2)
- Career Technical (2)
- Special Education School (4)
- Early College (1)
- Higher Education (2)
- Court/County School (2)

While many of these positions are principalships, it is important to include all of these responses into the survey sample size as it is assumed that administrators holding non-principal positions once held the job of principal and their background and experience should be validated. One respondent chose not to answer this question.

Overwhelmingly, 42.46 percent of respondents had served in the role of coach, while 29.19 percent had served as coachee. Two respondents chose not to answer this question.

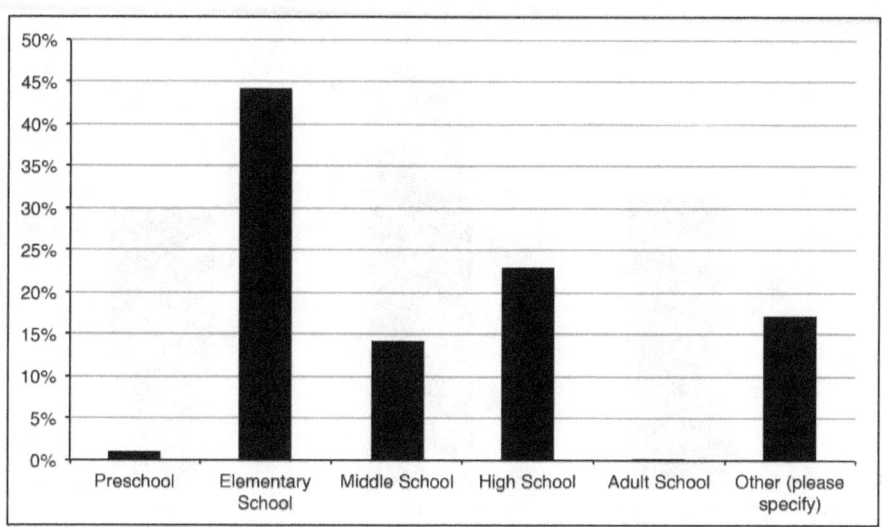

Figure 4.4. Current Administration Assignment.

For those who had participated in a coaching relationship, either as coach or coachee, a staggering 92.65 percent suggested it was an effective experience. Contrast this with only 7.35 percent indicating it was not effective.

In terms of surveying principals how they would value the experience of having a confidential coach, the response was clearly either highly valuable with 51.19 percent responding, and 29.31 percent valuable. Combine these results and the numbers are mind-blowing with 80.5 percent affirming coaching is considered either highly valuable or valuable by those who had experienced a coaching relationship.

CONSTRUCTED RESPONSE/OPEN-ENDED RESPONSES

The survey also contained two constructed response, or open-ended, items:

1. *What aspects of the coaching relationship made it effective?*
2. *What would have made the experience more effective?*

Surprisingly, there were a total of 953 responses provided by those surveyed.

1. *What aspects of the coaching relationship made it effective?* 473 individuals answered; 363 individuals skipped this question.

There were a number of themes that strongly emerged from respondents who experienced this relationship as either a coach or coachee. When asked

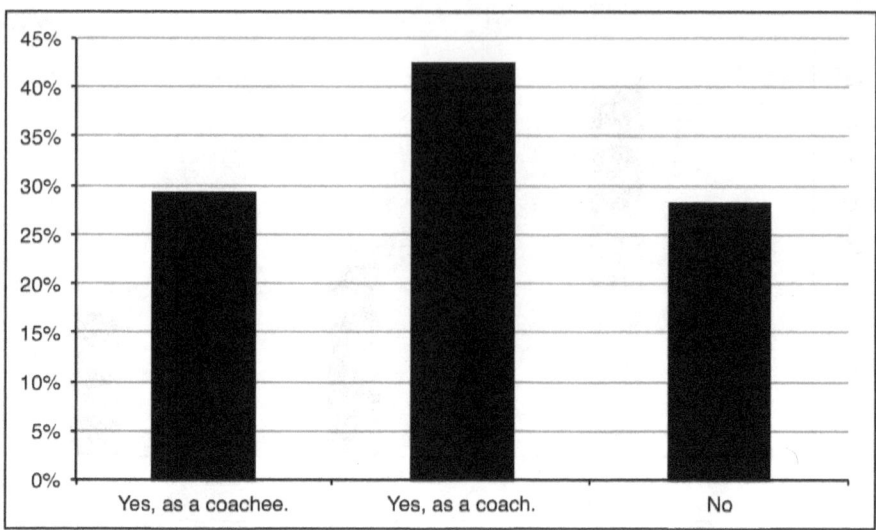

Figure 4.5. Participation in a Coaching Relationship.

to provide input on what aspects of that relationship made it a success, the following, in order of highest response, included:

Experience of the Coach

Overwhelmingly, both coaches and coachees agreed that the coach must have once held the position of principal. Responses included:

"Hearing the unique perspective of another administrator filtered through the lens of their own experience is particularly helpful."

"The connection with a veteran administrator coach that I could bounce ideas off of, or ask for input about an issue that the coach had likely faced before, was effective."

Moreover, the call for a successful coach to be a recent principal was important to many. One respondent stated the value of the relationship was having the "current, hands-on experiences and valuable professional experiences to share with a novice."

Goal Oriented

It all starts with a goal in mind. What is the purpose of this relationship and what will it lead to? This theme was suggested as a key characteristic of success within the coaching relationship. Responses supporting this included:

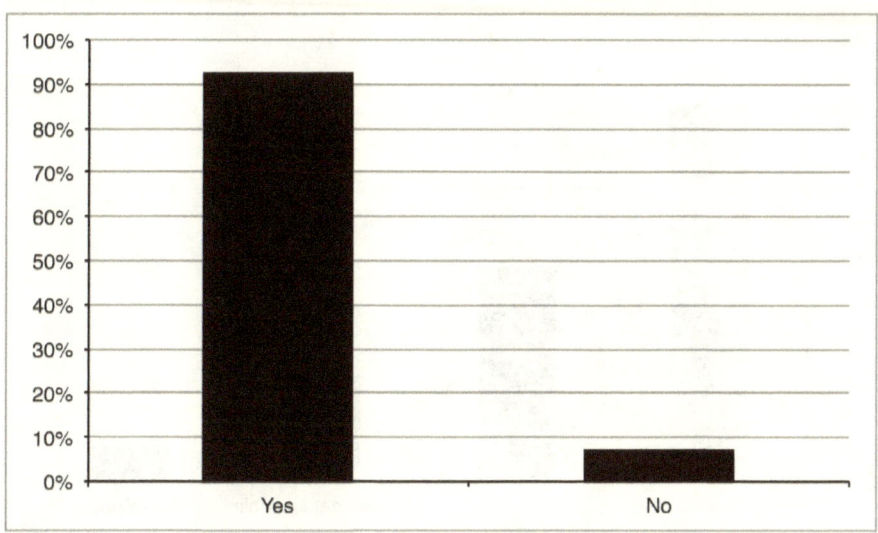

Figure 4.6.   Was the Coaching Relationship Effective?

"Real life, day-to-day examples of what a principal can expect. Things that cannot be taught in a classroom."

"Having a focus for learning and growth allows you to offer critical feedback that makes it about the work, and not the person."

"Having someone to guide you through the legal aspects of the job and having someone to bounce decisions off of before you made them and receive feedback as to the consequences of those decisions prior to making them."

"Coaching is an approach that helps the individual examine issues/concerns/problems through an inquiry process guided by the coach."

"Receiving direct feedback and areas I could work on. It was personalized so that I could develop a plan for improvement in those areas I needed to work on."

"Shared goals that were generated by the person being coached. The coach helped me to be reflective of the work, my reasons for doing the work, and the outcomes of the work."

A Confidential and Trusting Relationship

Overwhelmingly, respondents stated that having a confidential coach was of utmost importance. Being provided with unbiased, honest feedback without judgment was declared to be a must. Those comments included:

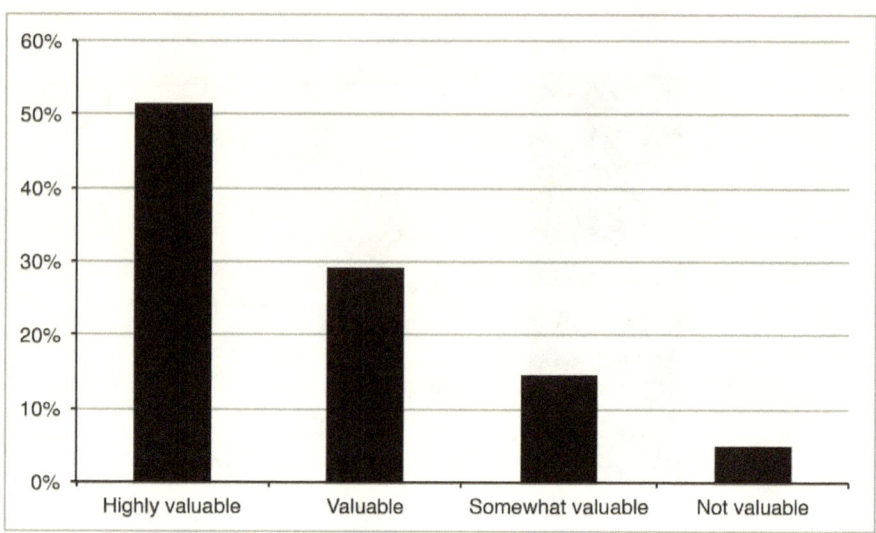

Figure 4.7. Value of a Confidential Coach.

"The coach was provided by the district, but did not work directly with my supervisor so the conversations could be more genuine."

"The coach did not work in the district, [but was] a consultant. So there was honest feedback without the fear of political retribution."

"The confidential nature and non-supervisory relationship made it easy for my coachee to ask questions and share concerns they may not have shared with their evaluator."

"Just having someone who did not belong to my district to hash some things out. Someone I could be truly honest with knowing that it would not affect my job status."

"It has been great to have someone I can trust with whom I can have full disclosure. No question is a 'dumb' question as the coach always had my best interest and development at heart."

Regularly Scheduled Meetings

Respondents were adamant that in order to have a successful coaching relationship, meetings between coach and coachee must be on a regular basis and face-to-face, which also included shadowing. This suggests that it makes the coaching experience more genuine and grounded in actual day-to-day reality. The responses for frequency ranged from weekly, bi-weekly, to monthly. Additionally, principals stated that the relationship should last multiple years with the same coach:

"The coaching was embedded into the school day and pointers were able to be given as immediate feedback."

"An effective coaching cycle included goal setting, plan a lesson, observe, discuss, refine, repeat."

"Regular collaboration helped calibrate and balance the needs of the district, school, and my own personal life."

Coach's Characteristics

Scores of responses provided centered on the characteristics or attributes of successful coaches. Most notably, feedback addressed the coach being available or on call, respectful, having a willingness to confront issues, collegial, motivating, understanding the context, well organized, and one who guides with intentional feedback. Specific responses on coaches' characteristics included:

"Frequent feedback on actionable strategies, rapport with the coach, respect between both parties, expertise on the part of the coach and a willingness to help the principal find my own way."

"They [the coach] worked to get to know my strengths, challenges, and areas for potential growth; they took a personal interest in my success."

"Having a caring heart, a listening ear, and reflective conversations made the relationship highly effective."

"Knowledge of current educational practice, appropriate research, effective listening strategies, and 'people' skills and insights are very helpful."

Non-evaluative

It was clear that the feedback provided here by administrators was for a coach-coachee relationship to be successful, working with a coach who was not their evaluator was key. Descriptors such as non-threatening, and comments like:

"I felt safe to make mistakes and could be honest in that risk-free environment."

"It was safe and I didn't feel like I was being evaluated or that anything negative would be passed on to my boss."

"Being able to ask questions that I didn't feel comfortable asking my evaluator."

Consistent Communication

Respondents cited the need for open, honest communication that centered on personal and real conversations. Feedback included the need for:

"Ongoing and consistent dialogue, open conversations about all administrative practices."

"Communication on a regular basis with challenges, questions, and accomplishments."

Strong Relationships

Those surveyed cited keys to success such as mutual respect between the parties, and having an open and honest dialogue, which leads to a strong coaching relationship. The coach/coachee relationship is unique, as one administrator stated:

"It is superior to a mentor-mentee relationship where the mentor generally is expected to provide the answers directly."

Another stated:

"[The coach] built a relationship with the principal which allowed for a greater understanding of the culture of the school."

Investment/Buy-In from Both Parties

Also important, according to those surveyed, included an investment into the relationship through collaboration, making a commitment to work together, and a deep concern for the coachee. That buy-in is critical and leads to:

"The ability to process important decisions with another person, talk freely about frustrations, and work to find solutions to administrative issues."

One-on-One Meetings

Also reported was the need for meetings to be one-on-one, not in a group setting:

"One-on-one face time allows for uninterrupted, designated time together."

"One-on-one contact throughout the course of the entire school year is critically important."

Improvement Was Evident

Responses also included recognizing that coaching paid off in improvement for the coachee such as:

"As I mentored a principal, I found that he often implemented what he learned to help his teaching practice. As a result, he became a more effective educator."

"I grew as an instructional leader by having a thought partner who allowed me to question my thinking in a safe environment without judgment."

"The coach improved my job performance as a result of the coaching relationship."

Coachee Characteristics

There were numerous suggestions from coaches as to what makes a successful coach. Those included a willingness to learn and ask questions, along with a positive attitude, which are obviously characteristics often seen in successful learners:

"The willingness of the mentee to learn all aspects of the principalship was motivating for us both."

"The ability to be coached through current issues/problems."

"A willingness [on the coachee] to take positive risks."

Coaches Networking

Coaches need support as well. This feedback was provided to support that notion:

"The most valuable aspect was learning from other veteran coaches in my district. I constantly asked them for suggestions for improvement on how I planned my practices and my leadership styles."

"The training that I received . . . to act as an induction coach gave me valuable tools to provide prospective administrators with."

2. *What would have made the experience more effective?* 480 individuals answered; 356 individuals skipped this question.

There were a number of themes that emerged from respondents who offered input on what aspects could have made their relationship more effective. The following, in order of highest response included:

More Time! More Coaching!

Over one-quarter of the responses was specific to wanting more time with their coach. Those who met monthly wanted bi-weekly. Those who had bi-weekly coaching wanted weekly. Also, respondents included feedback on wanting more years of having a coach. Again, it did not matter how many years they were coached, they just wished for more. Specifically, responses included:

"I would have liked more coaching with difficult situations—perhaps having her sit in on meetings, give feedback and share how I can improve. It was a lot of post-event feedback that would occur."

"More regularly scheduled meetings."

"Coaching sessions were hour per month. Twice a month would be desirable."

"More often—we meet about once a month—but sometimes it is only once every other month."

"There never seems to be enough time to drill as deep into the issues as I would like."

"A defined Coach that is regularly scheduled. Otherwise, everyone gets busy and weeks and months can fly by."

"I had the support for two years, which sounds sufficient, but at least one more year would have been more effective."

Experience of the Coach

Similar to the first open-ended question, administrators clearly stated here as well that it is critical to have a coach with experience as a principal and equally as important to have a recent practitioner. A sample of those responses to what would have made the relationship more effective were:

"Having someone that had more relevant experience. I had a retired principal who had been retired for some time. The info she provided was somewhat dated and didn't reflect the times."

"If I had someone who had been a principal more recently."

Also, some reported that the district should shoulder the load:

"If district had kept the coach up to date on latest requirements, tasks, responsibilities and systems."

Goals/Agenda

Again, having clear goals or an agenda were a key focus of this question:

"Having someone help model and coach me through things like school goals, budgeting, etc., would have been awesome."

"Mutually agreed upon and site-specific learning tasks would help make the experience more meaningful and effective."

"If the coach was more hands on, rather than just meeting/talking. In other words, show me, don't just tell me."

"I would have liked to have a coach to ask questions to but more importantly to have someone to help navigate the things that I did not know to ask."

"Working with the person on their school site. Walking their campus with them. Giving guidance on difficult situations."

Logistics

Interestingly, logistics of the coaching relationship became a theme among responses. Specifically, comments centered on meetings being site based, not over the phone:

"Time for on-site visits. I was appointed as a mentor for new principals, but checked in with them by phone for support as needed (not good)."

"If those times could have been face to face and more intentional."

For new principals, those logistics also included:
"It would have been more effective if the experience would have started as soon as the new principal was named."

Non-evaluative

Yet another recurring theme was the notion that the preferred coaching relationship should consist of the coach not being a position to evaluate the coachee:

"Being a principal can be very lonely, having to make difficult decisions on a daily basis. Having someone to calibrate decisions and get feedback in a non-judgmental manner on a regular basis is important."

"While I am not new to administration, I am new to the district. She [the coach] did not always keep everything I asked confidential, which was frustrating. She was trying to help, but I did not confide in her to tell others, merely to dialogue with her."

"Not sure if the coach was or was not reporting back to my boss made me a little guarded."

Coach as a Consultant

An intriguing number of responses suggested that coachees felt most comfortable if the coach was a paid consultant by the school district. A sample of those responses were:

"Knowing someone was being paid to be a coach would make the coachee feel more comfortable in taking time, asking questions and asking for help."

"Continuity with the coach. Over the years our district has used different consultants. Each consulting company brought a new set of coaches."

"When coaching ended, the principals wanted to continue the work, but with competing commitments and no longer having it as a 'requirement,' we stopped meeting, which is unfortunate . . . the quality of the meetings we had under a coach was very helpful to my professional growth."

Training

A few comments were in support of coaches receiving training to enhance the relationship:

"Resources to support the work that could have a positive effect on instruction."

"More training on how to coach and having difficult conversations."

Mandates

Some respondents indicated that while coaching was worthwhile, states and districts often inundated coachees with mandated paperwork:

"There were state requirements for paperwork that too away from coaching time."

"Too many assignments given by the state for us to complete that were not really very valuable to my growth."

Coachee Characteristics

Coachee characteristics was a recurring theme as well. A couple comments were:

"[A need for] a coachable individual, not looking for power and willingness and open-minded to ideas."

"Self-confidence on the part of the Coachee."

"Some participants are better able to self-reflect and refine practice [than others]."

Coach Characteristics

Coach characteristics also cycled back as a source of importance. Coachees stated:

"While I didn't expect to have answers given to me, I also didn't expect to listen to everything my coach had done in his previous life."

"More effective resources and tools [to support the coachee]."

Measure of Effectiveness

An unexpected theme suggested was to find a way to measure if the coaching relationship was beneficial:

"A valid performance evaluation tool [is needed]."

"In terms of being a coach, I think I will feel more effective as I improve my ability to share the growth I see when the areas . . . are not easily quantifiable."

"I have always been interested in finding out from my colleagues if I was making an improvement [because of coaching]."

Funding

Not surprising, the topic of funding surfaced. Clearly, a successful coaching model does come with a price tag. However, principals supported that expenditure:

"Prioritize funding for coaching."

"Sadly, the money behind the program was the biggest driving factor."

CONCLUSION

This robust study representing a large sample size of current principal practitioners has validated the premise of this book and also the literature stated prior. This survey adds to that body of literature, as well. Finally, it has provided school district leadership and researchers with valuable supportive evidence regarding the value and effectiveness of a principal coaching model in their organization.

Chapter Five

Case Studies

"If you always do what you've always done, you will always get what you've always got."
—Albert Einstein

This chapter will highlight three school districts representing unique and diverse areas of the country that have implemented a coaching model. The author was fortunate enough to spend time in each of these districts interviewing district leaders, coaches, and principals seeing firsthand their model of coaching their site principals. These models are a work in progress and not perfect. This is an attempt at offering examples of what other districts are doing around coaching.

These districts deserve praise for recognizing the need to support their principals with one-on-one coaching and we can certainly learn from them. The districts chosen for case studies were Tulsa Public Schools in Tulsa, Oklahoma; Downey Unified School District located in the Los Angeles suburb of Downey, California; and Hillsborough County Schools in Tampa, Florida. Two of these districts are remaking the traditional role of principal supervisor, allowing them to focus more deliberately on helping principals improve instruction in schools, while one district opted to hire an outside consultant to deliver the coaching product.

The following is a snapshot of each district including their demographic information, and a question and answer with district-level administration, coaches, and those principals being coached. Afterward, a glimpse into what the coaching conversations in these districts sounds like is provided.

CASE STUDY #1: TULSA PUBLIC SCHOOLS (TPS), TULSA, OKLAHOMA

School District Demographics

Coaching Model: Blended Model

Following the Blended Coaching Model of Bloom et al. (2005), one Instructional Leadership Director (ILD) says these phases in the TPS model include:

- Facilitative coaching, which includes feedback and reflective questioning
- Instructional, which focuses on her experience as a principal, advice, and resources, and
- Transformational, which includes interpersonal and communication skills, along with emotional intelligence leading to effective school leadership

Schools: 73 (K–12)
    Students 39,451
    High School Graduation Rate: 67 percent
    All principals are assigned an Instructional Leadership Director (i.e., Coach)
    7 ILDs serve all schools in "Networks"
    Frequency of coaching: 1–2 meetings monthly
    Coaching began in 2012

Questions and Answers

Participants: Dr. Errick Greene, Chief of Schools, ILD #1, ILD #2, Principal #1, and Principal #2

    Q: *How do you define the Tulsa Public Schools (TPS) coaching model?*

    Greene: The most direct support to principals is through the ILD through their constant communication either written, in-person, or via phone. They are folks who can bring some additional expertise to a particular crisis, an ongoing issue, implementation of a new initiative, thinking through student challenges, family challenges, or community challenges. Whatever it might be. We expect that the ILDs will provide that kind of guidance to principals.

    As a district, we really try to stress the need for ongoing learning. We actually have a theory of action that calls out being learners, contributors, and designers, all of us, serving in each of those roles at different times of the day, of the year. We want principals to be thinking about their constant areas for growth and that typically opens them up to learning new ideas and doing things better today than we did yesterday.

    Q: *Why was coaching launched in TPS?*

ILD #1: It was launched with the support of a grant from the Wallace Foundation. We made our connections through the Gates Foundation. We did a full district leadership study about five or six years ago and that leadership study indicated that the biggest gap between the work that we were doing and getting outcomes was the span of control between principals and Principal Supervisors. From that, the development of a new role, the Instructional Leadership Director, was created.

Prior to that, we didn't have anything for the Principal Coach. We had a Principal Supervisor and that Principal Supervisor for Elementary Schools was supervising 53 schools and 53 Principals. The Leadership Study indicated that we weren't getting any kind of traction out of that kind of support for principals. As a result of that, we were getting some coaching support from the Gates Foundation across different areas in the district in talent management, but this is an area [coaching] that just rose to the top in the study that needed attention.

Q: Describe the professional development ILDs receive.

Greene: We were with the Wallace Foundation for several years to develop our leadership pipeline and to deepen the school leader capacity to develop school leader managers, supervisors, and as we rethink how we at central office can best serve and support schools. Repositioning the district office as servants to the school with the school being the real unit of change in reaching and meeting student's needs.

If that is the case, we've got to situate ourselves in a way that doesn't always dictate to the school what they need, what they need to know, what resources they should have, et cetera, but to engage with them in more of a collaborative way than a top down model. That's what we're working hard to reconfigure and restructure. We're trying to at least ask more questions of principals.

ILD #1: ILDs and principals are trained together. The professional development focuses on three levers: observation and feedback, data driven instruction, and school culture.

Q: What is the primary challenge facing you as a principal?

Principal #1: Time. I think just the demands that we're given don't align with the time. I feel like TPS knows where they need to go and where we are putting our energy. Those are the things that are really change outcomes for kids. But the problem is, when I have 31 teachers, and 16 of those teachers are probationary, I get bogged down in just doing our observation system. It's really finding the time to do observations, the individual walk-throughs, and handling all the discipline in my building.

ILD #1: There's a much greater interest in accountability. The reason there's a much greater interest in accountability is that in Tulsa we haven't seen any measurable change in our student outcomes over the years. We need better outcomes for kids while we need principals with a pathway for developing their skills so they will have an impact on student performance.

We also know that principals won't learn and their practice doesn't improve if they aren't receiving a cycle of feedback so that they know if it's making a difference. Also, we have a really strong problem with teacher attrition. We lose a high percentage of teachers every year, especially in the first three years of teaching.

Q: From a principal's perspective, speak to the coaching relationship and the benefits you receive.

Principal #1: I would say it [coaching] is super helpful. In a big district you don't get lost. I was new to TPS when I came to be a principal so it's hard to be a first year principal, but it's also hard to be new in a district. My coach has really supported me in not getting lost but also helping grow my practice.

For example, if I am struggling with a parent, or I don't know how to work with a particular student or teacher, she can walk me through how to best handle the situation.

Principal #2: The ILD is my go-to person. It is really a coaching relationship. I don't ever feel like there's a harsh judgment or a "gotcha." It's more of a growth.

For a principal to have buy-in, it's to have somebody who can guide them, and in turn the principal is going to coach the teachers on those conversations. I can look her [ILD] dead in the eye and say, "I don't know. I'm at a loss," and I don't feel like she's going back to her office and getting on my evaluation and making notes. That's important because I don't think people can learn and grow in fear or on their heels, and I think that that's the most important thing. Just like with my teachers. I'm going to have to tread very carefully with them because I don't want them to feel like I'm out to get them.

I just want what's best for our kids here, so it's like trying to navigate those relationships can be tricky.

Q: How much time is spent coaching inside and outside the classroom during a coaching session?

Greene: We definitely ascribe to and push for a much greater percentage of the principal's time with the ILD focused on instructional leadership and something in the order of 75 to 80 percent although as a district we haven't specifically called that out.

ILD #1: About 30 percent. Our goal is eventually is to be beyond half. We have landed in a place where we have enough coaching experience and time with principals under our belts that we can see where our gaps are as Instructional Leadership Directors. We're digging deeper into norming our practices. Even though we've all been principals, we're a little different in our background. We bring some expertise to the table and we all have kind of different areas of interest and expertise that maybe the whole team can use.

Q: What is your greatest impact on the principals you coach?

ILD #1: I think that we've been able to focus the work so that principals can really get down to the business of determining whether or not they're getting results. I didn't have a measurable way to know or to be able to identify whether or not teacher practice was actually changing, except through test scores or outcomes for kids. The principal now monitors progress through analysis of student work and data.

ILD #2: Two areas: One is coaching around the feedback conversations and giving teachers feedback. If principals are able to do that well, then they're going to move the teacher's practice. The second area is coaching principals around some of the operational things that they need to learn how to do, but coaching them around the questions to ask in that process and thinking about what may seem an isolated thing, seeing how it all relates to support the teachers and the students. Principals have the tendency to hit everything a little bit and then consequently don't do any of it really well, so helping them narrow the scope and tying all of those pieces together. That's a different type of coaching. It's not necessarily instructional coaching but it ties together.

Q: Talk about how coaching led to a shift in district support.

Greene: There are additional supports on the network teams. These teams are directed by the ILD that include instructional coaches, special education coordinators, behavior coaches, talent management partners, and operations partners. All of these folks from around central office to help a network of schools to address issues that come up on a daily basis and if it weren't for that team, the principal's eye would be taken off of instruction and focused on many other things. Instead, they really maintain greater focus on teaching and learning.

Principal #1: We've organized our district offices in network support teams. The principal has the ability to tag other members of the team for support to her office staff or when it comes to budgeting and staffing talent management. Also, the network special education team here supports some compliance issues and also supports by coming on site when we have a really difficult kid and we're not sure what to do. We have the Instructional Coach providing support to myself and teachers, as well.

ILD #1: I meet with them once a month and coordinate the work. That's another aspect of my work besides directly with principals putting boots on the ground. They are deployed to the building to take those tasks off the plate of the principal so that their time is freed up to be in classrooms and be an instructional leader. All seven of the ILDs have our own team of people who just work with the schools that are in our network. For example, one special education coordinator is not covering 53 schools, they support the 12 schools in their network.

Q: How do you measure the effectiveness of your coaching model?

Greene: While we're seeing some promising sides in terms of some increasing graduation, definitely decreased negative and disruptive behaviors, some early signs of progress and pockets of excellence and promise here and there are those indicators. I'm still seeing and hearing some vestiges, some remnants of days past when there was a clear hierarchical punitive culture, where many of our leaders would expect to be told what to do and then follow that in a compliant nature.

We still fall into that from time to time when we get to these issues where there's no clear answer. We've engaged in more planning conversations, more innovation conversations. All of these things that I think continue to signal to school leaders that you've got tons of power and authority and opportunity to make this school community what it needs to be, and we need to hear from them so that we can better position ourselves to support you.

There are a good number who are really struggling with that because that's not how we've always operated and that's not what they grew up in as school leaders, and we are struggling to live up to that and respond to that in ways that are most effective and supportive of the school. It's a challenge to a system to be responsive in those ways.

Principal #2: You look at the teacher evaluation scores. I do some surveys in house from time to time about teacher satisfaction. Whenever people feel supported and somewhat encouraged to improve, I think the job satisfaction goes up. Also, student engagement in the classroom because teachers are receiving feedback to make them better, then you're going to have higher engagement in the classroom and less disruption because you're giving teachers those strategies to make a really effective class.

ILD #2: Success of the model starts with, is the principal doing this when I'm not there? Are they going in and looking at classrooms in the same way that we do? Also, are we seeing improvement in teacher practice? That can be either observed or that can be based on their evaluations. Then, is that translating into student achievement?

Another thing that is an important piece of data that sometimes we forget to look at in connection with this work is that discipline data because as the level of instruction goes up and the level of effectiveness of the teacher goes up and the student engagement goes up, you should see a decrease in certain classroom infractions that are a result of either kids being bored or kids being off-task or kids being non-engaged.

Q: How is the model funded?

Greene: Those foundations [Wallace and Gates] have supported more of the development. We have reconfigured, restructured our central office to create these roles. Our general funds are restructured in a way to try and make the organization a little flatter and to make sure that principals experience higher touch with their ILDs.

For example, easier access to them, increased communications with them and definitely with the support team members. Those support team members actually sit in other departments. That just forces our different departments to talk and to collaborate—really, forced conversations. It has forced us to think and work outside of silos. At some point, all of these folks are descending on the school which is trying to better facilitate and support principals so that more of their time is focused on the instructional program.

Q: Why is this model not more prevalent?

Greene: There's some age-old beliefs about how we do school. About how we structure and what that hierarchy looks like, and what it needs to be in order to operate effectively. Lots of tradition in that. My experiences taught me that there are many school leaders and former school leaders, now district leaders, who were amazing plant managers by keeping the buses running, lunch was efficiently served, and the building was generally run well, but not necessarily instructional leaders.

More and more we need to focus on instruction as society and therefore families and kids come to schools with more complex needs and we've got to think in a more complex way about meeting those needs. That requires more on the part of teachers and therefore different and more work on the part of school leaders. It's a requirement of the new work in educating our students. The silos have always been a challenge for districts. Not thinking more critically about how the work connects and how we can better connect it at the central office level in order to support schools.

We believe and are trying to live the belief that the school is the center of change, the unit of change for meeting students' needs and getting them to higher levels of proficiency, and that is driving more of our actions around supporting schools in different ways, in more differentiated ways. That requires of us to structure ourselves and to support and engage with schools in ways that are not the hierarchical. For example, talk to these five people before you can make this decision about buying a laptop or Chromebooks or whatever you need at your school. We've learned pretty quickly that in order for schools to be the nimble, agile, responsive organizations that they need to be, we as a larger organization need to be the same.

Q: If you were to recommend this model to a school district, what advice would you offer?

Greene: First, as a community, come to some consensus around what it means to be a principal in that culture, in that reality. Ultimately, where do you want to be in terms of how the school leader and the school leadership team and the school community lead out? How they think about ways to address student needs and how to communicate those with the rest of the district.

Then, think about the resources, oftentimes limited resources, that we have in a district in a central office and how might we decentralize as much of those resources out to schools so that school leaders actually have something to work with. That's really a challenge and it challenges lots of age-old beliefs about how we do school, but it's a must. Decentralizing as many of the resources as possible and that's probably going to be a phased approach.

Also, of your current pool of school leaders, what's the delta between where they are and where you want them to be? What's the coaching plan? What's the development? What are the experiences? What are the supports that they're going to need to get there? Understanding those, how are we or how can we be positioned to support them? Create a culture where it's expected that we're constantly learning from one another and we can set position aside to be open to learning and building our individual and collective capacity. The more we can help principals to self-assess accurately and identify their own needs, growth areas as well as areas of strength, and therefore areas where they need to be leading out with others.

Principal #2: Make sure coaches have the social, emotional intelligence and how to build those relationships [with coachees] and having the frame of mind of working with people, not on people. Then, having the principals in place and embrace it and want to do it and not made to feel like it is punitive.

ILD #1: It's a model that can be taught and can be learned but requires practice. We've had to have some coaching in order to be able to do that. I think if a coach can develop the skill to shift between different coaching stances in their work with the principal, I think you'll have the greatest probability of impacting their practice. For example, if ILDs were only coached to be directive and informational then I wouldn't expect that the skills of the principal would grow in any other way, except to just respond to compliance kinds of issues.

ILD #2: You have the right people in the place. You have to have a person that either has the skill set or you have to build the skill set in them in order for it to be effective. For me, I think it gives more of an instant credibility with principals if someone has sat in that seat. For coaches to be successful, they have to be able and willing to learn and be open and vulnerable to their own lack of knowledge. It's a two-way street. Coaches need to embrace that they don't have all the answers and that's okay. They have suggestions. They have experience. Coaches should be able to push their thinking to see things from different vantage points or all sides. Coaches have to be good at building relationships and building the trust.

CASE STUDY #2: DOWNEY UNIFIED SCHOOL DISTRICT, DOWNEY, CALIFORNIA

School District Demographics

Consultant Model: Multi-layered Approach
    Schools: 21 (K–12)
    Students: 22,782
    Frequency of coaching: 45 site/off-site meetings per school year
    Coaching began in: 2014
    High School Graduation Rate: 96 percent

Questions and Answers

Participants: Roger Brossmer, Assistant Supt-Secondary Education, Principal #1, Principal #2

Q: How do you define Downey's coaching model?
RB: This has been our Superintendent's vision. Prior to the Superintendent coming to Downey, we didn't have much in this area at all. This is a relatively new phenomenon for our district. It's running a district is through the principals. As a district office we strive to have a smoothly running district and support our school sites. We believe the magic happens in the classroom. Teachers are the first line and they make that happen, and principals are there to support them. We can't support all the teachers, but our job, central office, all the coaches, our job is to support those principals and help those principals.

The second part of our coaching are District Professional Learning Communities (PLCs). In groups of three to four, principals met with an assigned director (not supervisor). Being a principal can be a very lonely job. We don't want principals to feel alone and we want them to feel support, and so that was another mechanism by which we would support them so they felt like they had another advocate at the district office who wasn't their direct supervisor. Those directors had readings, or different leadership resources. It is more fluid and open. They meet on a monthly basis just to check in.

Another layer is that twice a month the instructional leadership team meets. Instructional leadership are all of those directors. A standing agenda item is, "Hey, how are your PLCs (Professional Learning Communities) going? If there's something going on, help make us aware of this. We're here to listen, what's going on?" This year, we morphed that into what we called trios (for elementary principals) and quads (for secondary).

This year we formed principal PLCs run by the principals themselves without a director present. There's an expectation of how many times they're going to meet, but what the idea is, who better knows your job than your peers? They know that they can invite directors or different people to come assist if they choose. One principal immediately set the tone by being real open. "Hey, I got this problem, I need your help." She was vulnerable. She was real with them, and she's not one to typically do that but she felt that she could be in that setting.

We kind of have these multiple paths. We have the big leadership, their outside coach if they've continued with it, and they have their trios or quads. That's kind of how we are doing our coaching model right now. Our goal is to support, fully support, our principals, then obviously coaching is a component of that overall philosophy.

Q: Why did Downey feel the need to hire a consultant to support its coaching model?

RB: We feel it's important that principals have a trusted ally outside the district, so if they're embarrassed or they don't want to talk about things we have that for them. Two years ago all principals had a coach, and with more support going to those newer principals. Then this year we gave veterans the option of having a coach. About half of them kept their coaches.

Also, we ensured that all of those new to the principalship along with new principals to the district are required to have a coach. Before our current Superintendent, certain principals got coaches and that wasn't because you were being successful. So we had to figure out, how do we bring back coaches without the stigma of, "You're messing up and you're in trouble"? We felt the safest way to do that is everyone gets a coach, so that's why we started with everyone. Now there's no stigma attached, and so now we have that.

Q: Why was coaching launched in Downey?

RB: It really it started with our Superintendent and his prior experience with this model. That was part of when he came in. He had a vision of what he wanted to do, and he just slowly rolled it out, but then he's also been very open to transitioning and modifying as needed for us. If your philosophy is, "We run the district through principals," I think this is just really an outcome of that philosophy.

Q: How often and does the consultant provide feedback?

RB: We'll meet on a quarterly basis to report out. However, the consultant can pick up the phone and call if there's a concern. There's no formal feedback.

Q: What is the primary challenge facing you as a principal?

Principal #1: My primary challenge as a principal is to change culture at my site. My particular site has a veteran staff and a reputation of many continuation schools in that it is for the "bad" kids. I am actively working to change that perception and ensure that pathways to all post–high school options exist. I feel that the coach I have is a great sounding board who offers years of culture-changing experience both at the school site as well as in the community.

Principal #2: The primary challenge is staying focused on instruction. There are many distractions that if you don't handle and take care of they can explode. Extracurricular issues have been a challenge for me—this year it has been cheerleading, last year it was the band. Parent conferences, school discipline, community wants and needs, teacher parking, tardies, and trash are other examples.

Q: From the principal's perspective, speak to the coaching relationship and the benefits received.

RB: We don't want to betray the trust between the consultant coach and the principal. Being a principal is a tough job, and we understand that and we'll support you, but at the end of the day, we may have to choose to go a different direction. Can we look each other in the face and say, "Did we give that principal everything we could to help them?" We will support them, but that doesn't necessarily mean they are going to be successful. If not, it won't be for lack of district support.

Principal #1: I receive the benefit of my coach's experience as an administrator coupled with the promise of a privileged relationship in which ideas and challenges can be freely shared. I currently receive more than five visits per school year and my coach is available by phone anytime.

Principal #2: Being a high school principal can be a lonely job. Sometimes you need to "bounce" items off of someone who can give you guidance and/or support that is not at the site or district level. Being a principal you are "caught in the middle." For example, I do not like saying the district is making us do this or that, or if I am having an issue at the site I don't want to call the district because they at times make a relatively small matter into a big one.

Q: How much time is spent inside and outside of the classroom during a coaching session?

Principal #1: The amount of time spent in classrooms is dependent on what I want to work on. I can virtually spend our entire session in classrooms if necessary. Usually our sessions are about two hours long.

Principal #2: When we first started coaching the model, we [the coach and I] spent the majority of time walking the school and observing classes and talking about instruction and the implementation of the instructional focus. Now the majority of time is spent with me individually as well as with the entire administrative team.

Q: Talk about how coaching led to a shift in district support.

RB: The principals absolutely love the trios and quads. We have combined principals meeting, and then we have segments where elementary and secondary principals are sometimes meeting separately. Each monthly meeting has professional development, along with quad and trio debriefs that are part of our leadership strand. The strands are data-driven instruction, integration of technology and learning, and leadership-moving from being a manager to an instructional leader.

They have moved from principal meetings being all business that could have really been done in the e-mail. In between each meeting, we have the district instructional team meeting. There's an administrative-only part where they talk about the next combined and segment meetings. They have principal representatives on the district instructional leadership team to get their input.

There was a generous general consensus that the professional development was not meeting the principal's needs as they didn't see the connection. This year we really worked hard making sure we're being explicit about those connections, and they feel like they have a voice in that. Those topics come from the bottom up.

Q: How do you see the model evolving?

RB: I would foresee a time that principal meetings will all be at the school site and part of those meetings will be visitations. We would be on each other's sites and really help each other out. I don't think we're there yet. I'd like to see where principals are going into classrooms with each other and having those conversations, not in isolation, but actually on the sites.

Q: How do you measure effectiveness of your coaching model?

RB: I don't think we have any real tangible way. I think it's more of some of the intangibles. Are they feeling supported? Are the schools running well? If you were to say, "Principals, do you feel supported?" They would say "yes" because there's a huge feeling the district is there to help us, not just put more stuff on our plate.

We do have the feedback sessions with the coaches, so we meet with the coaches. If there's a real hot-button issue, we can address that, but I don't think we have a formal mechanism by which to do that. This year we will require all of our principals to do an anonymous survey of their teachers in and around a level of support. Now, as part of that, we are also going to be surveyed by them.

Q: How is the model funded and how much does the consultant cost?

RB: That was something that we support as a district, and we actually pay through our state funds. In terms of cost, coaching is one part of a contract that includes other services. The coaching component of that contract is roughly $96,000 per year.

Q: Why is the model not more prevalent?

RB: I think we always try to in-house stuff in education. Just because we all started as a teachers, what makes us think we all have MBAs. It's just this whole lack of acknowledgment that we don't have strengths in all these other areas, and the best way to do it is don't try to in-house it, go to the pros. I think it's just that reluctantly, whether it be a financial consideration, "Oh we can't spend money on that." Or just a lack of general acknowledgment that there's real pros out there, and I just think it's been frowned upon in education. We always just try to in-house it, and I think that's where we go wrong.

Q: If you were to recommend this model to a school district, what advice would you offer?

RB: Establish the "why" for the need to coach principals. It's not one more thing. Make sure that you're very transparently clear on the why. The growth mindset that we can always do better. That, as a principal, why would we treat our principals as any other profession that there's no assumption that once you have the job, you have it all wired. Our job is too hard, too complicated. The idea is that even successful principals can benefit from a coach.

CASE STUDY #3: HILLSBOROUGH COUNTY SCHOOLS, TAMPA, FLORIDA

School District Demographics

Coaching Model: Blended Model
   Schools: 250 (P–12)
   Students: 206,841
   Year 1–2 principals are coached in an induction method
   Year ≥3 principals are coached on an as requested basis
   8 Principal Coaches District-wide
   Frequency of coaching 1–2 times monthly
   Coaching began in 2010
   Data of HS grad rate 82.2 percent

Questions and Answers

Participants: Kim Huff, Director of Principal Pipeline, Principal Coach #1 (PC #1), Principal Coach #2 (PC #2), Principal #1, and Principal #2, District Director #1 (DD #1), and District Director #2 (DD #2)

Q: How do you define the Hillsborough County Schools coaching model?

Huff: I would define it as supporting and pushing the practice of beginning principals and also adding to their knowledge of best practices.

Q: Why was coaching launched in Hillsborough?

Huff: It started out with the Wallace Foundation. When we were looking at our Principal Pipeline, we were looking at our year one and two principals and thought that they needed more support so we did two things. One, with the grant money we hired principal coaches for just year one and two principals. Two, we were then trained as coaches on content and coaching.

Then we also started our Principal Induction Program. That also was some additional coursework for those year ones and twos to continue to learn once they were in the job. The coaches also manage those trainings. The data that came back from principal surveys was how valuable those principals felt the coaches were and how valuable that work is for them. Today, the district has actually taken over the cost of the program.

Q: Describe the professional development Principal Coaches receive.

Huff: We attended the blended coaching training, but then we also spent two years being coached ourselves by the New Teacher Center. They would come out and observe us out in the field and provide a forum of opportunity and learning for us. Then we would observe each other. We also did a lot of observing. We would observe a principal facilitating a leadership team meeting or a faculty meeting and then give them feedback.

We all have been certified as coaches. Also, our district and our leadership development have been phenomenal about also sending us almost anywhere we wanted to go to enhance our own learning. We attend conferences and different trainings, and then we bring back and we share with our coaches.

In addition, coaches have a forum every quarter that builds on our own professional learning. Then we have a coaches' retreat every summer that focuses on enhancing our own learning. So it's a constant. It's definitely a group of learners, and I think what is really important to all of us is that we continue to grow and get better.

PC #1: We first had an initial three-day training through the New Teacher Center. We learned about blended coaching. We also learned about facilitative or instructional coaching. In terms of ongoing professional development, we are provided opportunities where we can travel and learn more. Another very important professional development I receive is that as coaches we typically try to shadow each other once a month. They come out in the field, they take anecdotal notes, we debrief immediately after, and they give me feedback. They basically coach me on my coaching. Those models I find are very helpful as well. Also, we also hold coaches' forums twice a year where we as a coaching community decide on a topic and then we come together learning. We also hold every other week a coaches' Professional Learning Community (PLC). We typically will present a problem of practice during that coach PLC where, again, all the coaches at the table are helping that one coach through whatever that problem of practice is.

Q: How has the principalship changed in recent years?

PC #1: It has changed so dramatically. When we first became principals, let's say again ten years ago or fifteen years ago, a lot of emphasis was on the management of the building, making sure that the facility was in top shape, making sure that your master schedule was up and running and people were adhering to it. You, of course, had the hiring and firing of staff members, whether it be a teacher or paraprofessional. You attended lots of different meetings with different stakeholder groups. You were a little bit more of the lone decision maker. It was kind of your domain, your area, your expertise. You kind of ran the show.

That has shifted so much in terms of really now your number one position is to be the instructional leader and the instructional voice within the building, really leading the charge on what quality teaching looks like, having your pulse on student learning and student outcomes and what are the barriers to the student outcomes and can I help you as a team or a grade level or a school remove those barriers. Also, being able to speak intelligently about best practices and being able to have the ability to coach staff members to help them come to their own level of learning, their next steps that they feel comfortable implementing, being able to cycle back and see those next steps in action.

There is much more collaborative emphasis on building up and training and supporting teacher leaders, maximizing leadership opportunities for staff members, really being, again, the first coach to your assistant principal, coaching them through scenarios. You've really shifted roles into being viewed now as the lead learner and that instructional visionary at the site.

Our system was that if you were a satisfactory teacher I had to formally observe you once every three years. It's astounding how frequently we're in the classrooms now giving bite size chunks of feedback, that just right just in time feedback.

Q: From a principal's perspective, speak to the coaching relationship and the benefits you receive.

Principal #1: My coach is someone to sound off to. She has incredible expertise and she sees things I don't. My coach provides me with support and help, especially when I'm down. I'm not sure what I would do without her. I can have discussions with her that I could not have with others. She is always there for me. Always has my back.

DD #1: When I was a principal, my coach was like my thought partner through everything that I was doing. She would sit in. My whole staff knew that she existed and existed only for me. She would talk me through the reflection of whatever she observed. Also, for example, if I needed resources, I would say, "I'm looking for some behavior systems in the school."

My coach would share everything from all of her coaching and her own personal principal experience. I never started from the ground. I always had different things I could pick from as far as getting started. It was constant. We would walk through the campus together. It was having somebody on the side of me like a Mini-Me who could guide me. The trust factor was so high. Her skills helped me think about what I was doing, and not direct me, and not make judgments, but the thought of what I was doing was powerful.

Principal #2: Having a coach has been valuable. It is an outside perspective. As principals we often have tunnel vision and a different sense of reality. She makes me think.

Q: How much time is spent coaching inside and outside the classroom during a coaching session?

Huff: We haven't quantified that. As a coach, you do some work out in the classrooms, but I wouldn't say the majority of our time. A lot of time might be spent on culture building. It might be spent on evaluations, or on how to give feedback. It could be spent on how to share their vision.

The coaching is based more on the principal's goals which are based off our competencies. For each of the principals you coach, you know what those are. You have them, so that really leads the direction of your coaching with that principal. So if you have a principal that really needed support in getting into the classrooms and getting feedback, then the coach could certainly apply. It's really differentiated for each principal and each school.

Q: What is your greatest impact on the principals you coach?

PC #1: My greatest impact is helping principals expand their ability to think through problems and their ability to think through and expand their capacity on leadership. My number one role or priority is to help that principal expand their capacity to be a more effective leader.

PC #2: I help principals with the thought process which includes guiding their thinking, suggesting ideas, next steps, and providing resources to support that. I am someone they can talk to—a "thought partner." I can pull research for them if necessary to help them close the gap between instructional practice and student achievement.

Q: How do you measure the effectiveness of your coaching model?

Huff: We measure the effectiveness of our model by looking at the principals who have been coached. We looked at their top scores for their particular school as well as their evaluation to see the before and after. Both data are very positive. That also gave us a little bit of a catalyst for making the coaching positions, once the grant ran out, be permanent positions.

DD #1: At the end of this year, we're going from eight coaches down to four, which speaks to retention of principals. We don't need a whole lot of coaches anymore because the principals are staying, they're doing a pretty good job, and so we whittled down the number of coaches that are in those roles. As we see student performance hopefully begin to rise, we should begin to see the fruits of that investment.

PC #1: I think with everything we do, whether it's professional development or whether it's coaching, ultimately was it successful and did what we coach around stick? When I open up my coaching sessions with my principals we typically start by cycling back to the previous session. I try to monitor or evaluate if what we've spoken about was in fact implemented or vetted out or thought through.

We also do some periodic small surveys to see if their practice has changed throughout the year. I feel like I'm responsible for helping their practice change. I also measure some success on student outcomes. We do give an end-of-the-year coaching survey and give it out a little more informally.

Q: How is the model funded?

Huff: It comes out of our general funds but we're looking to reduce the number of coaches from eight to four. There are eight coaches in Hillsborough to serve each area. What we're going to do in Hillsborough is hire an area deputy superintendent for each area to close that span of control and then go back to four coaches. Four coaches can definitely handle the workload of just year one and two principals coaching. We're going to go back to that really being their main focus [first and second year principals].

Q: Why is this model not more prevalent?

Huff: In education in general in our country, we're so slow to change and change our model of how we do things. Coaching is just one example of that. Yes, it's financial, and we haven't done it before, so people aren't willing to. I just think people are very difficult to change, and they don't. So they choose not to. It's easier not to change.

I know that even as a veteran principal myself, when I was a principal, I would have loved to have had a coach. Being a principal is a very isolating job. I just think it's a systemic problem and that we're slow to change unfortunately.

DD #1: I think it has a lot to do with where people view what is going to have the greatest impact on students. I think our superintendent has focused on leadership being the lever to improve schools.

Even if you have great teachers, if you don't have great leaders who are going to get them to perform together as one unit, then they're not effective. We've got to make great investments in the principal in order to get to where we're trying to go. Some people don't recognize that as the key lever as we have, which is why the investment then looks different when you look at the budget. You talk about $1 million into leadership and support for just those first and second year principals, that's because of that focus. It was investment worth making.

DD #2: Only recently, say the last five to eight years, people really started talking about the importance of the principal role in supporting and developing teachers in the building. There's always been great teachers, but then it goes back to that idea of pockets of excellence again. Sometimes there are great teachers, and there's always going to be sometimes great teachers despite the fact that they might have a principal who's not very good. The support for understanding how important the leader of the school is evident by the fact that it was written into federal law. I think that there's all of a sudden real conscious awareness of how important the leaders are in schools today.

Q: If you were to recommend this model to a school district, what advice would you offer?

Huff: I think it is really important to have an outside expert come in and help train your principal coaches. I also think if they can go and observe another district's practice to see what's happening there, if they can go and observe and hear about a program elsewhere and the effect that it has.

Also, I would probably start small. We started small then we got big. It's a work in progress because it's a fairly new position, so we're constantly recognizing [that] the support that you can give a principal and make them so much more effective in their job right out of the gate is definitely worth the investment. I guess I would start small, and I would rely on the experts and, if possible, I would try to go and see some coaching in other districts.

DD #1: We started with the coaches working with first and second year principals, and they were focused on them. I felt that I had a coach because she came often, she supported, she mentored, she guided, and I could call her. She wasn't overtaxed.

We then had the evolved model where they began working with area superintendents, they began taking on every principal from experienced to brand new, and we're now shifting back. Now we're going back to where we started, which is not having them with every principal. It's taken them back to focusing solely on first and second year principals so that they feel that intimate coaching and support that was so successful in the beginning. I would say stick to it and find something else for those veteran folks.

DD #2: If a school district is only going to do one thing, I think that you do it. I think that you figure out how many coaches you need, what would their workload be, and how do we support these brand new principals, because it accelerates the learning curve of the administrators. Whether it's assistant principals who are new or principals who are new, the response has always been very positive. They felt like the relationship and what they got out of it really helped them do their job better faster.

COACHING CONVERSATIONS: WHAT DOES IT SOUND LIKE?

On this particular day, the high school began the coaching conversation with the principal by asking, "What will be today's focus?" The principal responded by asking for support with a teacher who is having some issues failing too many students and is also having challenges with classroom management. In addition, she wanted some coaching around how to push a strong teacher, who even though is outstanding, to do better, to "tighten up" some of her practices. Next, the coach and coachee headed out to visit those classrooms. After visiting the first teacher's classroom, the coach and principal debriefed in the hallway.

The coach asked, "What did you see?"

The principal responded by mentioning positives such as all students had materials and used technology (Smartboard). Next, she mentioned that the teacher was asking questions that did not appear to be scripted and while the students were asked to take notes, less than a quarter were actually doing so.

The coach then pressed, "What might it look like if the teacher had prepared questions scripted out and as a result, who would be doing the heavy lifting [of the work, i.e., students should be]?"

Just as the principal began to answer, the coach asked, "What would it [that conversation with the teacher] sound like?" The two then engaged in a role play of that conversation with the coach taking the position of the veteran teacher who is often reluctant to receive feedback. Afterward, the coach advised, "Relationship building with this teacher needs to come first."

In terms of the large number of students failing that teacher's class, she coached the principal to have a conversation that would "focus on the big picture and drill down from there. How many students are not passing? How can we get them to move on?"

She added, "When talking with her [the teacher] begin with compliments, such as students on task and each had materials. If the teacher names the issue, they will own it."

Then the coach asked, "When do you think you can have this conversation with her?"

"In the next week," replied the principal.

"Great. Email me how it goes."

As one can see, the coaching conversations were powerful for the simple reason of role playing. The principal received action steps. Difficult conversations can be uncomfortable, but with the support of the coach, the principal has the opportunity to test-drive that conversation before the real one takes place. Additionally, it was impressive to see the accountability within that coaching relationship. The coach did not leave or move on after the role play; they pressed and asked the coachee when they planned on having the conversation and to send the coach a follow-up email on how things went.

On this afternoon, a Principal Coach and the Principal Coachee are debriefing an Instructional Leadership Team (ILT) meeting in which the Principal Coach observed. The principal asked her coach to provide feedback on how she can improve the meetings. Here is the debrief of that observation, which focuses on the line of questioning and statements posed by the Principal Coach:

Principal Coach: "What were your initial thoughts about the meeting?"

Principal Coach: She then offered, "I noticed . . ."

Principal Coach: Then, "I wondered . . ."

Principal Coach: Next, she moved into offering a suggestion. "Perhaps your conversations at the meeting would be deeper if they [the team] had the data prior to the meeting. What do you think of that?"

Principal Coach: Then, she asked a clarifying question. "What have you done to prep teachers as to what the function of ILT really is?"

Principal: "Nothing."

Principal Coach: "Perhaps you could revisit that."

Principal: "Yes. I could."

Principal Coach: Next she offered a suggestion. "Perhaps you could do a fishbowl activity at your next staff meeting to show what the ILT looks like."

Principal Coach: She then goes a little deeper with a clarifying question. "Your expectation is for the ILT to carry back the information to their PLCs. How could you roll that out?"

Principal: "I don't know."

Principal Coach: She offers another suggestion.

Principal: "I think that will work. Thank you."

Principal Coach: She revisits the conversation and asks, "Regarding next steps, what is your plan for the future [around this topic]?"

Clearly, this was an honest conversation in a risk-free environment created by the coach with the added accountability piece of next steps.

CONCLUSION

These three districts provide unique and different approaches to principal coaching and as a result make excellent case studies. There are pieces of each that are supported by research, the survey conducted in this book, and those coaching elements worthy of being non-negotiables. There may also be some aspects that are not supported by the research and the like. Regardless, what we should learn from Tulsa, Downey, and Hillsborough is that:

- district leadership value their principals,
- their leadership courageously took the risk and had a vision to do what they know and believe is outstanding support for their principals,
- their principals are being coached in these districts,
- they began with what they believed worked best for their organization and have retooled along the way,
- through qualitative and quantitative data, principal coaching is making a difference in the way principals feel valued and supported, and its positive impact on student performance,
- they have not abandoned principal coaching even in the face of economic challenges or political pressures,
- principal coaching is a component of how they do business in those districts. Kudos to them for leading the way for those of us who want to embark on a similar journey because we too see the value in providing principals with coaching.

Chapter Six

Best Practices, Proven Results, and Next Steps

> *"Teaching players during practices was what coaching was all about to me."*
> —John Wooden

This chapter will focus on providing practitioners with best practices in order to successfully plan, design, and implement a coaching program or to enhance the one already in place in their school district through best practices. In addition, it will highlight proven results of this coaching model.

RESEARCH-BASED IMPLEMENTATION MODEL (RBIM)

Table 6.1 is a depiction of the ideal model of a coaching program based upon the research from experts (chapter 3, "What the Literature Says"), the in-depth administrator survey conducted for this book (chapter 4, "What the Principals Have to Say"), and from the case studies learned earlier (chapter 5, "Case Studies"). The Research-Based Implementation Model (RBIM) can be used for implementing a coaching model in school districts today.

One component of the RBIM is "non-negotiables." These are the must-haves for a coaching program to be successful. The RBIM's non-negotiables are a destination. A goal. Perhaps it is a place where a district or administrative team might want to arrive as a district with a coaching model. However, as we learned from the case studies in chapter 5, implementation is differentiated. Perhaps not all of these non-negotiables are feasible at the outset and that is acceptable. What is important is that a district begin the journey of a coaching program or fine-tune its current one.

Table 6.1. Research-Based Implementation Model (RBIM)

Non-negotiables	Optional Practices
District support	Include assistant principals
Coach experience as a principal	Induction/on-boarding model
Confidentiality and trust	Benchmark peer organizations
Coachee-driven agenda	
One-on-one interactions	
Regularly scheduled meetings	
Ongoing professional development for coaches	
Goals, outcomes, and planning	
Classroom observation	
Compensation for coaches	

Be mindful that what works in one school district may not work in another. Three unique models of implementing a coaching program were described in chapter 5 ("Case Studies") and each reported success using their own definition. Regardless of the approach, what is required is courageous top-level leadership to implement these practices. Find what works for your organization and run with it.

NON-NEGOTIABLES

District Support

A successful model is more than just assigning a coach to a principal. The district's central office must provide layered support, as well. The example learned from Tulsa Public Schools is a perfect case of building the capacity within the organization to truly support principals. Their model consists of additional supports on their network teams and those teams take direction from the Instructional Leadership Director (coach) as to what support a principal may need.

Those supports include instructional coaches, special education coordinators, behavior coaches, talent management partners, or operations partners. These central office departments help a network of schools to address issues that come up on a daily basis, which helps the principal to maintain greater focus on teaching and learning.

Coach Experience as a Principal

Certainly, one thing learned from the principal survey is that principals want to be coached by those who have themselves held the position of principal at one time in their career. This makes sense. No one would expect a major league baseball hitting coach to provide batting tips if they never once stepped to the plate themselves. The same applies here.

Additionally, being a recent or current practitioner is critical due to the fact, as we read in chapter 3, "What the Literature Says," the job has changed so much in recent years that someone who has been out of the position for some time will not be as effective as one who possesses that current experience unless they stay current.

Confidentiality and Trust

Perhaps the most seminal of the best practices is the idea that in order for a coach and coachee to have a meaningful and successful relationship, confidentiality and trust is paramount. They must go hand in hand. This was heard over and over. Trust and confidentiality are critical.

Confidentiality leads to trust, which provides the coachee with a risk-free environment to share without the concern of the conversation being reported back to a supervisor, or the threat of evaluation of being tied to the relationship. While that model does seemingly work in Tulsa Public Schools, they might just be an outlier. In short, principals without a confidential relationship reported that while they valued their coach, they could not be 100 percent open and honest with the idea that what they may share could be passed up the ladder.

Coachee-Driven Agenda

Coinciding with the notion of trust, principals who have been in a coaching relationship agree that successful coaching includes the coachee driving the majority of the agenda. Who better to know what the challenges principals are facing than the coachee themselves? If they feel trust in their coach, they are more likely to open up and address current issues while hoping for real solutions. Certainly, a skilled coach may introduce areas they see as challenges as well. However, the coachee needs to be setting most of the agenda for the coaching session. After all, it is for them.

One-on-One Interactions

Regardless of some research studies supporting the model of group coaching, the findings of this study support a one-on-one coaching model. One-on-one is believed to be the most effective. This was a best practice learned through the principal survey and case studies. Also, it clearly ties into the idea mentioned earlier of confidentiality and trust. How can a coaching relationship be confidential and centered on trust when there are other coachees in the room? Most principals would not feel comfortable and be open and forthright with the challenges they are facing with others listening into their conversation. Additionally, often in a group setting, one member typically dominates the conversation, which leaves others out and unable to be heard.

In addition, creating a solid relationship between coach and coachee takes time and effort. That is a challenging enough dynamic. It is asking a great deal to assume that one coach and multiple coachees will all have successfully functional relationships.

Regularly Scheduled Meetings

In chapter 4, "What the Principals Have to Say," the data from the author's nationwide principal survey was described and reported. When asked, *What would have made the experience more effective*? recall that overwhelmingly responses came through about the desire for more coaching time and more regularly scheduled meetings. Obviously, being a principal is a busy job. However, these principals were willing to make time for coaching. Principal coaching needs to be a priority in order to help them navigate the challenges of the position.

One solution is to calendar all meetings and schedule them regularly. Principals are slaves to their calendar and if something is calendared, most likely they will be there. Each district should define what works for their principals and their organization's budget as to the definition of regularly. Based on the research, at minimum, monthly meetings should be scheduled during the instructional day.

Ongoing Professional Development for Coaches

In chapter 5, "Case Studies," exemplary school districts that implemented a coaching model with the intent to support their principals were highlighted. In order to support their site leaders, these districts realized that their coaches needed up-front and ongoing professional development. Each had a successful and unique method of providing their coaches with professional development that ranged from in-house models to consultants and even self-selected opportunities. Ongoing professional development is a must as coaches look to improve their impact on their coachees. It was imperative for them to stay relevant with current practices in the field.

Goals, Outcomes, and Planning

As the research indicated in chapter 3, along with the survey results in chapter 4, critical components to sustaining improved practice for principals, coaches, and coachees must focus on goals, anticipated outcomes, and next steps or action planning for follow-up. One respondent stated the success of their coaching relationship: "There was mutual trust and an intentional focus on improving instruction and building relationships." The successful coach-coachee relationship needs a roadmap and setting goals accomplishes that.

Additionally, progress monitoring of those goals, evaluating the results, and creating actionable next steps, which hold both parties accountable, is critical for success.

Classroom Observation

While it is critical to support principals in dealing with the day-to-day challenges of the job, it is important to include classroom walk-throughs as a component to the coaching visit. Supporting teachers and improving student performance should be the ultimate focus. As we learned from our case studies, these districts valued the practice of coach and coachee observing teachers and students in classroom settings. However, none were specific as to the expectation of how much time should be spent observing classrooms during coaching meetings. Regardless, districts should include walk-throughs and determine what works best for their organization.

Compensation for Coaches

Regardless if a district chooses an in-house model or hires a consultant, there needs to be a line item budgeted for this endeavor. Survey respondents stated that knowing someone was being paid to be a coach would make the coachee feel more comfortable in taking time, asking questions, and asking for help. Often in education, we try to take the shortcut and add responsibilities onto the backs of administration.

Regardless, coaches should be compensated. As we saw in two case studies, Tulsa and Hillsborough, they built the internal capacity for their model that included restructuring titles and responsibilities. In Downey, they opted for the outside expert to come in and support their principals. Again, there is no right or wrong way here as long as coaches receive compensation for their services.

OPTIONAL PRACTICES FOR CONSIDERATION

Table 6.1 also is a depiction of optional practices for consideration. Often all the "non-negotiables" described above of an ideal model of a coaching program may not all be a feasible or a complete list for a school district. As a result, this section of the chapter introduces a few optional practices, which may either be implemented as stand-alone initiatives or complementary to those "non-negotiables" listed above.

Include Assistant Principals

If monetary and coaching resources permit, districts could decide to deepen its coaching capacity and include its assistant principals. For example, Hillsborough County Schools in Tampa, Florida, has such a model. Not only do principals in their first and second years receive regularly scheduled coaching, but so do their assistant principals as a component to its Assistant Principal Induction Program.

Once an administrator becomes an assistant principal, they receive coaching over a three-year period. This is just one aspect of their Principal Pipeline, which is an excellent model for building internal capacity, cultivating their own talent, and supporting them in the position through ongoing coaching.

Induction/On-boarding Model

While all principals should have a coach, that might not be feasible for school districts. Initially, districts may find it financially challenging to supply each principal a coach. As a compromise, districts may choose to implement a model that at the outset supports those in the first few years in the position. It is recommended that at minimum, principals in their first three years should have a coach. This concept of induction, or on-boarding, should be considered an optional implementation model to get a coaching program off the ground.

In chapter 5, we saw examples of two districts that approached this concept differently. Downey Unified began its coaching program with a coach being deployed to each principal, and in year two regrettably scaled back to only include those principals in the first two years on the job and those who opted in to having a coach, while Hillsborough County Schools has mostly maintained the induction model.

Benchmarking Peer Organizations

Earlier, Hillsborough County Schools offered the suggestion of going to observe another district's practice prior to implementation. Another way to define this exercise is benchmarking. Benchmarking refers to learning models and best practices of peer organizations, which is another optional practice. Tucker (1996) describes benchmarking as a data-driven and research-based step-by-step guideline for increasing effectiveness in an organization. As an optional practice, two relatable components of her guideline include locating organizations that exemplify an ideal coaching model, and two, considering an on-site visit to that particular school district.

COACHING TYPES

Obviously, a great deal of time has been spent in this book, and specifically in this chapter, describing the benefits of coaching and best practices for implementation. What should also be considered important are two high-leverage forms of coaching: *Blended* and *Cognitive*. Both have a place in a successful coaching relationship and here are the definitions of both and their value.

Blended Coaching

Chapter 5 provided examples of districts using Blended Coaching as a coaching method. Bloom et al. (2003) believe that effective leadership coaching is supported by their Blended Coaching Strategies. The authors define this approach as being composed of two coaching roles. "The coach may play a facilitative role, guiding the coachee to learning through the use of feedback and reflective questions. At other times, the coach may play an instructional role and provide expert information, advice, and resources" (Bloom et al., 2008, p. 8).

As you will see, there is value in having a specific coaching method that is situationally dictated. Specifically, Bloom et al. (2008) provide examples of both the facilitative and instructional approaches and how they support the coachee to achieve their goals. There is a specific time and place for each. For example, the facilitative approach may support coachees internalizing their learning through strategies such as reflection, analysis, or the coach observing the coachee on the job (Bloom et al., 2008).

Moreover, the facilitative method could be simply offering feedback on the coachee's interactions and asking them to reflect on their practice (Bloom et al., 2008). Bloom et al. (2008) call this *"ways of being."* As for the instructional approach, that focuses on *"ways of doing,"* which typically centers on more direct feedback that could include time management strategies (Bloom et al., 2008).

Cognitive Coaching

Cognitive Coaching is a process during which one explores the thinking behind their practices. The relevance of Cognitive Coaching in relation to principals receiving coaching is Cognitive Coaching suggests that a person seems to maintain a cognitive map, which is only partially conscious. As a result, in Cognitive Coaching, principal coaches ask questions that are designed to reveal to the principal areas of that map that may not be complete or consciously developed. If the relationship between coach and coachee is strong, corrective feedback may also be a component of Cognitive Coaching as well.

How is this accomplished? According to Costa and Garmston (1994), a cognitive coach uses reflective questioning, which includes paraphrasing, pausing, and probing for specifics. A cognitive coach helps another person "to develop expertise in planning, reflecting, problem-solving, and decision-making. These are the invisible tools of being a professional, and they are the source of all teachers' choices and behaviors" (Costa & Garmston, 1994, p. 13).

Additionally, Barnett and O'Mahony (2006) suggest that in order to guide a person to self-directed learning, this coaching model requires the coach to be nonjudgmental, and to encourage reflective practice. Barnett and O'Mahony (2006) assert in order to encourage reflection, cognitive coaching focuses on one's thinking, assumptions, beliefs, and perceptions, and how these impact one's practices.

In the RBIM, a skilled cognitive coach would spend time with the principal, collecting data that leads to posing questions to engage the principal in reflective thinking (Barnett & O'Mahony, 2006). The payoff, according to the researchers, is by becoming more reflective about their practice, educational leaders will be better-informed decision makers.

PROVEN RESULTS

To this point, decision makers in school districts most likely are in agreement that their principals would benefit greatly from the coaching model presented here. However, the lingering question might be, *Does it work*? It is a fair question, considering the resources that must be invested in order to implement coaching in their district. The following results show significant gains in student performance for three schools over a three-year period. The author had the pleasure of serving as the principal coach for the three principal leaders of these schools.

The coaching model followed the RBIM non-negotiables. Of particular note was the success at Wailuku Elementary School (figure 6.1) and Waihee Elementary School (figure 6.2), which were high poverty (Title I) schools.

Figure 6.3 shows the success at Kamali'i Elementary School, which is a non–Title I school and often these types of schools are equally challenging to improve student performance.

The data were taken from the Hawaii Content and Performance Standards (HCPS III) state assessment from 2004–2005 and the ending in 2006–2007. Students in grades three and five were assessed in both language arts and mathematics. As the data suggests, dramatic gains were made in these content areas.

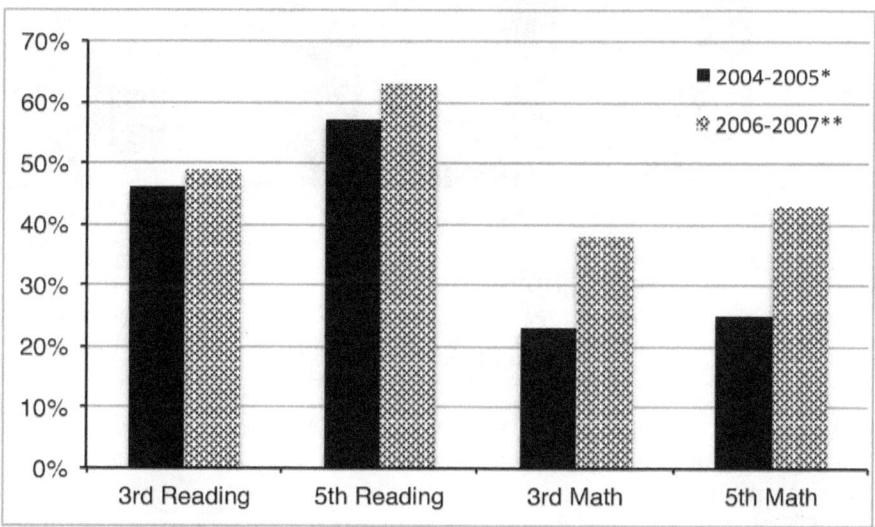

Figure 6.1. Wailuku Elementary HCPS III.

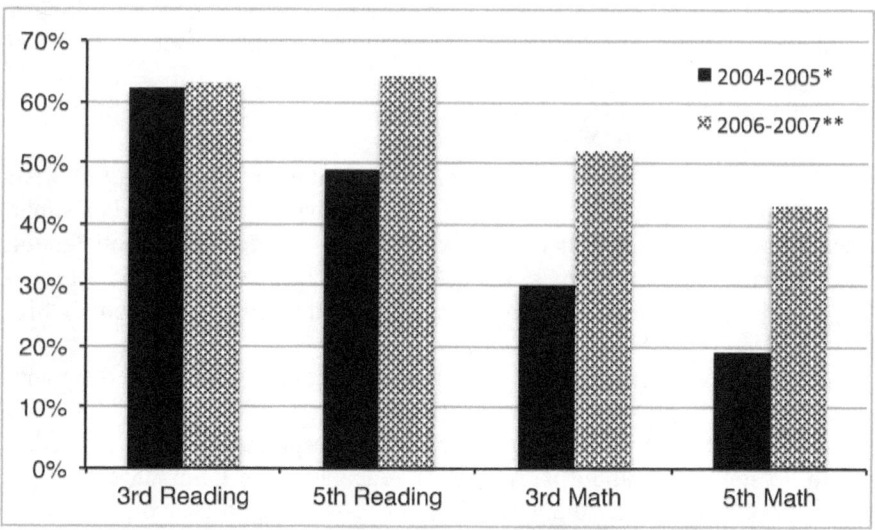

Figure 6.2. Waihee Elementary HCPS III.

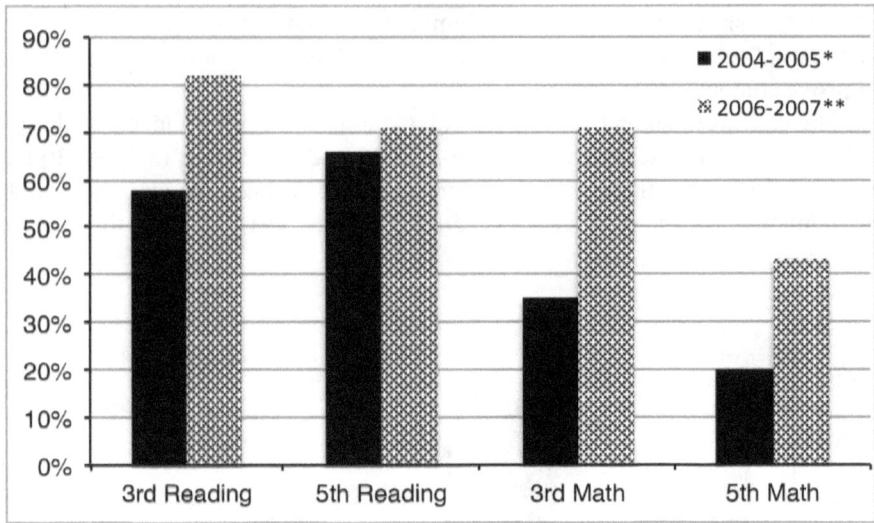

Figure 6.3. Kamali'i Elementary HCPS III.

PUTTING IT ALL TOGETHER

Looking back at chapter 1, "It's Lonely in the Middle," the goals for this book were to present the hypothesis that today's principalship is a lonely position and one that has become increasingly demanding in recent years, and coaching was the mechanism to support principals to deal with these stressors. Next, the author presented literature to support his hypothesis, then surveyed current principals to give them a voice as to what coaching does or could mean to them, highlighted three exemplary school districts with different coaching models, and finally put it all together in a Research-Based Implementation Model for school districts use as a roadmap for implementation.

Educators are often too quick to put other things in place ahead of what has been acknowledged here. Investing in coaching for principals is a sound research-based endeavor that can pay dividends in greater job satisfaction and performance of principals, increased student achievement, and a reduction on principal turnover, leading to healthier bottom lines for school district budgets.

This book should be a call to action to school district leadership that supporting their principals matters. Districts must acknowledge that their principals are craving this support and need it desperately, and in turn commit to do something about it. A goal of education is to help students reach their potential by giving them all of the necessary supports, which not only should include outstanding teachers in the classroom, but also principals who have the skill set and resources to support what happens in the classroom. Coaching accomplishes that. Go slow to go fast, but get going. Your principals await.

References

Aas, M. (2016). Leaders as learners: Developing new leadership practices. *Professional Development in Education*, 1–15.

Aas, M., and Vavik, M. (2015). Group coaching: A new way of constructing leadership identity? *School Leadership & Management*, *35*(3), 251–265.

Association of California School Administrators (ACSA). (2016, August 1). Coaching needed to build leaders. *Education California*.

Bacon, T. R., & Spear, K. I. (2003). *Adaptive coaching: The art and practice of a client-centered approach to performance improvement*. Palo Alto, CA: Davis-Black.

Baker, B. D., Punswick, E., and Belt, C. (2010). School leadership stability, principal moves, and departures: Evidence from Missouri. *Educational Administration Quarterly, 46*(4), 523–557. doi:10.1177/0013161X10383832.

Barnett, B. G., and O'Mahony, G. R. (2006). Developing a culture of reflection: Implications for school improvement. *Reflective practice*, *7*(4), 499–523.

Battle, D., and Gruber, K. (2010). Principal attrition and mobility: Results from the 2008–09 principal follow-up survey (NCES 2010-337). National Center for Education Statistics, Institute of Education Sciences, U.S. Department of Education. Washington, DC: US Government Printing Office.

Bell, C. (2000, February). The mentor as partner. *Training and Development*, 52–56.

Béteille, T., Kalogrides, D., and Loeb, S. (2012). Stepping stones: Principal career paths and school outcomes. *Social Science Research, 41*(4), 904–919. doi:10.1016/j.ssresearch.2012.03.003

Bickman, L., Goldring, E., De Andrade, A. R., Breda, C., and Goff, P. (2012). Improving principal leadership through feedback and coaching. *Society for Research on Educational Effectiveness*.

Bloom, G., Castagna, C., Moir, E., and Warren, B. (2005). *Blended coaching: Skills and strategies to support principal development*. New York: Sage.

Bloom, G., Castagna, C., and Warren, B. (2003). More than mentors: Principal coaching. *Leadership, 32*(5), 20–30.

Bossi, M. (2007). Revolutionary Leadership. *Leadership, 36*(5), 32–34, 36–38.

Bossi, M. (2008). Does leadership coaching really work? *Leadership, 38*(1), 31–36.

Boyce, J., and Bowers, A. J. (2016). Principal turnover: Are there different types of principals who move from or leave their schools? A latent class analysis of the 2007–2008 Schools and Staffing Survey and the 2008–2009 Principal Follow-Up Survey. *Leadership and Policy in Schools*, 1–36.

References

Branch, G. F., Hanushek, E. A., and Rivkin, S. G. (2012). *Estimating the effect of leaders on public sector productivity: The case of school principals* (No. w17803). Cambridge, MA: National Bureau of Economic Research.

Browne-Ferrigno, T., and Muth, R. (2006). Leadership mentoring and situated learning: Catalysts for principalship readiness and lifelong mentoring. *Mentoring and Tutoring, 14*, 275–295.

Bush, T. (2009). Leadership development and school improvement: Contemporary issues in leadership development. *Educational Review, 61*(4), 375–389.

Bush, T., Glover, D., and Harris, A. (2007). *Review of school leadership development.* Nottingham, UK: National College for School Leadership.

Carruthers, J. (1993). The principles and practice of mentoring. In B. Caldwell and E. Carter (Eds.), *The return of the mentor: Strategies for workplace learning.* London, England: Falmer Press.

Clotfelter, C., Ladd, H. F., Vigdor, J., and Wheeler, J. (2006). High poverty schools and the distribution of teachers and principals. Sanford Working Paper Series. SAN06-08. Sanford School of Public Policy Durham, NC.

Clutterbuck, D., and Megginson, D. (1999). *Mentoring executives and directors.* Oxford: Butterworth-Heinemann.

Costa, A. L., and Garmston, R. J. (1994). *Cognitive coaching: A foundation for renaissance schools.* Norwood, MA: Christopher-Gordon Publishers, Inc.

Covey, S. R., Merrill, A. R., and Merrill, R. R. (1995). *First things first.* New York: Simon and Schuster.

Crow, G. M. (1992). The principalship as a career: In need of a theory. *Educational Management & Administration, 20*(2), 80–87.

Crow, G. (2006). Complexity and the beginning principal in the United States: Perspectives on socialisation. *Journal of Educational Administration, 44*(4), 310–325.

Crow, G. and Matthews, L. J. (1998). *Finding one's way: How mentoring can lead to dynamic leadership.* Thousand Oaks, CA: Corwin Press.

Cullen, J. B., and Mazzeo, M. J. (2008). Implicit performance awards: An empirical analysis of the labor market for public school administrators. San Diego, CA: University of California.

Cunard, R. (2017) *Successful principal: Concrete strategies and essential advice.* Lanham, MD: Rowman & Littlefield.

Danielson, C., and McGreal, T. L. (2000). *Teacher evaluation to enhance professional practice.* Alexandria, VA: ASCD.

Daresh, J. C. (2004). Mentoring school leaders: Professional promise or predictable problems? *Educational Administration Quarterly, 40*(4), 495–517.

Daresh, J., and T. Male. (2000). Crossing the boundary into leadership: Experiences of newly appointed British headteachers and American principals. *Educational Management and Administration 28*(1), 89–101.

Darling-Hammond, L. (2010). *The flat world and education: How America's commitment to equity will determine our future.* New York: Teachers College Press.

DeAngelis, K. J., and White, B. R. (2011). Principal turnover in Illinois public schools, 2001–2008. Policy Research: IERC 2011-1. Edwardsville, IL: Illinois Education Research Council.

Ed Source. (2015, July 16). J. Fensterwald. Half of new teachers quit profession in 5 years? Not true, new study says.

Educational Research Service. (2000). The principal, keystone of a high-achieving school: Attracting and keeping the leaders we need. Arlington, VA.

Farley-Ripple, E. N., Raffel, J. A., and Welch, J. C. (2012). Administrator career paths and decision processes. *Journal of Educational Administration, 50*(6), 788–816.

Fink, E., and Resnik, L. (2001, April). Developing principals as instructional leaders. *Phi Delta Kappan, 82*(8), 598–606.

Flaherty, J. (2005). *Coaching: Evoking excellence in others.* Burlington, MA: Butterworth-Heinemann.

Friedman, T. (2005). *The world is flat.* New York: Farrar, Straus and Giroux.

Fritts, P. J. (1998). *The new managerial mentor.* Mountain View, CA: Davies-Black Pub.

Fullan, M. (2008). *What's worth fighting for in the principalship* (2nd ed.). New York: Teachers' College Press.
Fuller, E. J., and Young, M. D. (2009). Tenure and retention of newly hired principals in Texas. University Council for Educational Administration, Department of Educational Administration, University of Texas at Austin.
Gates, S. M., Guarino, C. M., Santibañez, L., and Ghosh-Dastidar, B. (2004). *The careers of public school administrators*. Santa Monica, CA: RAND Education.
Hallinger, P. (2011). Leadership for learning: Lessons from 40 years of empirical research. *Journal of Educational Administration, 49*(2), 125–142.
Hallinger, P., and Heck, R. (1996). Reassessing the principal's role in school effectiveness: A review of empirical research, 1980–1995. *Educational Administration Quarterly, 32*(1), 5–44.
Hallinger, P., and Heck, R. (2009). Assessing the contributions of distributed leadership to school improvement. *American Education Research Journal, 46*(3), 626–658.
Hansford, B., and Ehrich, L. (2005). The principalship: How significant is mentoring? *Journal of Educational Administration, 44*(1), 36–52.
Hargrove, R. (2008). *Masterful coaching*. San Francisco, CA: Jossey-Bass/Pfeiffer.
Hayashi, C. A. (2016). Administrative coaching practices: Content, personalization, and support. *Educational Leadership and Administration, 27,* 173–197.
Heifetz, R. and Linsky, M. (2002). *Leadership on the line: Staying alive through the dangers of leading*. Boston, MA: Harvard Business School Publishing.
Houle, J. C. (2006, February). Professional development for urban principals in underperforming schools. *Education and Urban Society, 38*(2), 142–159.
Huff, J., Preston, C., and Goldring, E. (2013). Implementation of a coaching program for school principals: Evaluating coaches' strategies and the results. *Educational Management Administration & Leadership, 41*(4), 504–526.
James-Ward, C. (2011). The development of an infrastructure for a model of coaching principals. *International Journal of Educational Leadership Preparation, 6*(1), n1.
Johnson, L. A. (2005). Why principals quit: There are many reasons why principals voluntarily leave the positions they worked so hard to earn. *Principal, 84*(3), 21–23.
Kilburg, R. R. (1996). Towards a conceptual understanding and definition of executive coaching. *Consulting Psychology Journal 48*(2), 134–144.
Killion, J. (2012). Coaching in the K–12 context. In J. Fletcher and C. A. Mullen (Eds.), *The SAGE handbook of mentoring and coaching in education* (pp. 273–295). Thousand Oaks, CA: Sage.
Killion, J., and Harrison, C. (2006). *Taking the lead: New roles for teachers and school-based coaches*. Oxford, OH: National Staff Development Council.
Koonce, R. (1994). One on one: Executive coaching for underperforming top-level managers. *Training and Development, 48*(2), 34–40.
Kram, K. (1988). *Mentoring at work: Developmental relationships in organisational life*. Lanham, MD: University Press of America.
Leithwood, K., Harris, A., and Hopkins, D. (2008). Seven strong claims about successful school leadership. *School Leadership & Management, 28*(1), 27–42.
Leithwood, K., and Louis, K. S. (2012). *Linking leadership to student learning*. San Francisco, CA: Jossey-Bass.
Lochmiller, C. R. (2013). Leadership coaching in an induction program for novice principals: A 3-year study. *Journal of Research on Leadership Education, 9*(1), 59–84, https://doi.org/10.11771942775113502020.
Lochmiller, C. R. (2014). What would it cost to coach every new principal? An estimate using statewide personnel data. *Education Policy Analysis Archives, 22*(55).
Louis, K. S., Leithwood, K., Wahlstrom, K. L., Anderson, S. E., Michlin, M., & Mascall, B. (2010). Learning from leadership: Investigating the links to improved student learning. *Center for Applied Research and Educational Improvement/University of Minnesota and Ontario Institute for Studies in Education/University of Toronto, 42,* 50.

References

Marzano, R., Waters, T., and McNulty, B. (2005). *School leadership that works: From research to results*. Alexandria, VA: Association for Supervision and Curriculum Development.

Mavrogordato, M., and Cannon, M. (2009). Coaching principals: A model for leadership development. Paper presented at the annual conference of the University Counsel of Educational Administration, Anaheim, CA, 19–22 November 2009.

Mendels, P., and Mitgang, L. (2013). Creating strong principals. *Educational Leadership, 70*(7), 22–29.

Miller, A. (2013). Principal turnover and student achievement. *Economics of Education Review, 36*, 60–72.

Mitgang, L. (2012). *The making of the principal: Five lessons in leadership training*. New York: The Wallace Foundation. Retrieved from http://www.wallacefoundation.org/knowledge-center/school-leadership/effective-principal-leadership/Documents/The-Making-of-the-Principal-Five-Lessons-in-Leadership-Training.pdf.

National Policy Board for Educational Administration (NPBEA). (2002). *Instructions to implement standards for advanced programs in educational leadership for principals, superintendents, curriculum directors and supervisors*. Arlington, VA: Author.

Northouse, P. G. (2007). *Leadership: Theories and practices*. Thousand Oaks, CA: Sage.

Novak, D., Reilly, M., and Williams, D. (2010). Leadership practices accelerate into high speed. *The Journal of the National Staff Development Council, 31*(3), 32–37.

Odden, A. R. (Ed.). (2009). *10 strategies for doubling student performance*. Thousand Oaks, CA: Corwin Press.

Rhodes, C. (2012). Mentoring and coaching for leadership development in schools. In S. J. Fletcher and C. A. Mullen (Eds.), *The SAGE handbook of mentoring and coaching in education* (243–256). Thousand Oaks, CA: Sage.

Rich, R. A., and Jackson, S. H. (2005). Peer coaching: Principals learning from principals; Pairing novice and experienced principals provides both with opportunities to promote reflective thinking in their decision-making. *Principal, 84*(5), 30–33.

Roberts, A. (2000). Mentoring revisited: A phenomenological reading of the literature. *Mentoring and Tutoring, 8*(2), 145–170.

Smith, A. A. (2007). Mentoring for experienced school principals: Professional learning in a safe place. *Mentoring & Tutoring, 15*(3), 277–291.

Sousa, D. A. (2016). *How the brain learns*. Thousand Oaks, CA: Corwin Press.

Stein, S. J., and Gewirtzman, L. (2003). *Principal training on the ground: Ensuring highly qualified leadership*. Portsmouth, NH: Heinemann.

Stickel, S. (2005, March 17). PDD Item 03 April 2005 - Information Memoranda (State Board of Education) Department of Education, The Principal Training Program: Instructional Leader Coaches Option Assembly Bill 164. Retrieved from California Department of Education: http://www2.cde.ca.gov/scripts/texis.exe/webinator.

Tucker, P. D., Young, M. D., and Koschoreck, J. W. (2012). Leading research-based change in educational leadership preparation: An introduction. *Journal of Research on Leadership Education, 7*(2), 155–171.

Tucker, S. (1996). *Benchmarking: A guide for educators*. Thousand Oaks, CA: Corwin Press.

Villani, S. (2005). *Mentoring and induction programs that support new principals*. Thousand Oaks, CA: Corwin Press.

Warren, S. R., and Kelsen, V. E. (2013). Leadership coaching: Building the capacity of urban principals in underperforming schools. *Journal of Urban Learning, Teaching, and Research, 9*, 18–31.

Weinstein, M., Jacobowitz, R., Ely, T., Landon, K., and Schwartz, A. E. (2009). *New schools, new leaders: A study of principal turnover and academic achievement at new high schools in New York City*. New York: The Institute for Education and Social Policy, New York University.

Wise, D. (2010). School leadership coaching: What does it look like? *International Journal of Educational Leadership Preparation, 5*(1), 1–6.

Witziers, B., Bosker, R. J., and Krüger, M. L. (2003). Educational leadership and student achievement: The elusive search for an association. *Educational Administration Quarterly*, *39*(3), 398–425.

Young, M. D., Crow, G. M., Murphy, J., and Ogawa, R. T. (Eds.). (2009). *Handbook of research on the education of school leaders*. New York: Routledge.

Zepeda, S. J. (2014). *The principal as instructional leader: A handbook for supervisors*. New York: Routledge.

About the Author

Dr. **Larry Hausner** has been an educator for over twenty years. His first career was a sportscaster. Most notably, he was the host and executive producer of *Sports Spotlight*, a weekly talk show on Sports Channel (today Fox Sports). In addition, he was the play-by-voice of numerous minor league baseball teams, including the Honolulu Sharks and Hilo Stars of the Hawaii Winter Baseball League.

His career in education began as a teacher in the Orange Unified School District. After three years of teaching he became assistant principal at the same school. After serving in this capacity for two years, he was selected as the principal of the school where over 70 percent of the students were English language learners and over 80 percent qualified for the free and reduced lunch program. Dr. Hausner later served as principal at two other schools in the district along with being the administrative director. Currently, he serves in the Saddleback Valley Unified School District as a site principal.

Additionally, Dr. Hausner has served as adjunct professor of education for the past thirteen years. Today, he is associate professor of education at the University of Southern California in the Doctorate of Education program. His doctorate is in K–12 leadership in urban school settings and was earned at the University of Southern California in the same program in which he teaches.

He is the founder of Coaching School Leadership (www.coachingschoolleadership.com), a consulting firm dedicated to supporting principals through coaching.

Dr. Hausner is an avid sports fan and resides in Southern California with his children, Riley and Jacob.

www.ingramcontent.com/pod-product-compliance
Lightning Source LLC
Chambersburg PA
CBHW021801230426
43669CB00006B/154